Reading
Student
Writing

Reading Student Writing

Confessions,
Meditations,
and Rants

Lad Tobin

Boynton/Cook • HEINEMANN • Portsmouth, NH

Boynton/Cook Publishers, Inc.
A subsidiary of Reed Elsevier Inc.
361 Hanover Street
Portsmouth, NH 03801–3912
www.boyntoncook.com

Offices and agents throughout the world

The author and publisher wish to thank those who have generously given permission to reprint borrowed material:

"Car Wrecks, Baseball Caps, and Man-to-Man Defense: The Personal Narrative of Adolescent Males" by Lad Tobin originally appeared in *College English* 58 (1996). Copyright © 1996 by the National Council of Teachers of English. Reprinted with permission of the publisher.

"Reading and Writing About Death, Disease, and Dysfunction; or How I've Spent My Summer Vacations" by Lad Tobin originally appeared in *Narration as Knowledge: Tales of the Teaching Life* edited by Joseph F. Trimmer. Copyright © 1997 by Boynton/Cook Publishers. Reprinted with permission of the publisher.

"Teaching Against the Teaching Against Pedagogy: Reading Our Classrooms, Writing Our Selves" by Lad Tobin originally appeared in the journal *Reader: Essays in Reader-Oriented Theory, Criticism, and Pedagogy*, Vol. 33/34, Spring/Fall 1995. Reprinted by permission of University of Pittsburgh Press.

"You Are Invited . . . to Leave" by Lad Tobin originally appeared in the journal *The Fourth Genre: Explorations in Nonfiction*, Vol. 1, No. 2, 1999. Reprinted by permission of Michigan State University Press.

Library of Congress Cataloging-in-Publication Data
Tobin, Lad.
  Reading student writing : confessions, meditations, and rants / Lad Tobin.
    p. cm.
  Includes bibliographical references.
  ISBN 0-86709-545-8 (alk. paper)
  1. English language—Rhetoric—Study and teaching.   2. Report writing—Study and teaching (Higher).   3. College students' writings—Evaluation.   4. Report writing—Ability testing. 5. College prose—Evaluation.   I. Title.

PE1404.T625 2004
808'.042'0711—dc22   2004000562

Editor: Lisa Luedeke
Production: Vicki Kasabian
Cover design: Night & Day Design
Typesetter: Publishers' Design and Production Services, Inc.
Manufacturing: Steve Bernier

Printed in the United States of America on acid-free paper
08 07 06 05 04   VP   1 2 3 4 5

Contents

ACKNOWLEDGMENTS   vii

PROLOGUE: *You're Invited to Leave (But I'd Really Rather You Stayed)*   1

INTRODUCTION: *The Elephant in the Classroom*   7

PART 1   READING STUDENT WRITING

1   How Many Writing Teachers Does It Take to Read a Student Essay?   17

2   Reading and Writing About Death, Disease, and Dysfunction, or How I Spend My Summer Vacations   31

3   Replacing the Carrot with the Couch: Reading Psychotherapeutically   44

4   Car Wrecks, Baseball Caps, and Man-to-Man Defense: The Personal Narratives of Adolescent Males   56

PART 2   READING OURSELVES AS WRITING TEACHERS

5   Fear and Loathing of Fear and Loathing: Analyzing Our Love-Hate Relationship with Emotion   76

6   Referring Ourselves to the Counseling Center: Confronting Boredom and Burnout in the Teaching of Writing   86

7   Teaching with a Fake ID   95

PART 3	READING THE TEACHING OF WRITING

8   Reading Composition's Misplaced Anxieties About Personal Writing   105

9   What We're Walling In, What We're Walling Out: Reading (and Rewriting) Our Own Bad Assignments   116

10   Reading Our Classrooms, Writing Our Selves   127

WORKS CITED   141

Acknowledgments

I've received wise advice and generous support on this project from some of the best writers and teachers I know. Randy Albers, Bruce Ballenger, Eileen Donovan-Kranz, Mary Rose O'Reilley, Libby Rankin, and Michael Steinberg all talked with me over many years about the ideas in this book, as did my late and dear friends, Wendy Bishop, Bob Connors, and Dan Sheridan.

Diana Cruz, Beth Dacey, Eileen Donovan-Kranz, Paul Lewis, Jim Smith, Jeff Tobin, Joe Tobin, and Chris Wilson all provided crucial assistance with Chapter 1, "How Many Writing Teachers Does It Take to Read a Student Essay?" And, in writing Chapter 7, "Teaching with a Fake ID," I got very useful feedback from Sarah Grover, Rebecca Ingalls, Sue Johndrow, Paula Mathieu, Staci Shultz, and Tim Lindgren.

Tom Newkirk's remarkable scholarship on reading student writing has informed my own work from the time I first entered the field; I am enormously grateful to Tom for helping me with all aspects of this project, from listening to me sort out the initial ideas while we hiked in the White Mountains to giving me perceptive and detailed suggestions on the final manuscript. I'm grateful, too, to Paula Salvio who also read much of this book in manuscript and who gave me just the support and suggestions I needed to keep going.

I owe thanks to everyone at Heinemann Boynton/Cook, but particularly to Vicki Kasabian who quickly and expertly guided this book through the production process; to my copy editor, Alan Huisman, whose unerringly skillful and elegant changes improved this book in immeasurable ways; and to my editor, Lisa Luedeke, who had the wisdom to know the sort of book I was trying to write before I did and who gave me just the right mix of guidance and freedom along the way (I should confess that Lisa gave me more and longer extensions than I've ever given to any of my first-year students).

The readers I trust and care about most—my daughters, Lucy Tobin and Emma Tobin, and my wife, Toby Gordon—gave me the motivation and encouragement to complete this book, even when I tried to talk them out of it. My brother, Dan, and father-in-law, Fred Gordon, read some of this work in progress and were very helpful in important ways. And I don't think that I've ever fully acknowledged just how much both of my parents have influenced the way I seem to read everything, including student essays.

Finally, I am grateful to all of the students I've taught over the past twelve years at Boston College. If they hadn't written all those essays, I could not have written this book. Of course, if they hadn't made those essays quite so provocative, I might not have needed all those extensions.

Prologue
You're Invited to Leave
(But I'd Really Rather You Stayed)

When I was in eighth grade, I used to spend a lot of time after school playing pick-up basketball in Jeremy Rosenstein's driveway. It was a good place to play—walking distance from school, a basket that was a few inches less than regulation height, and several younger Rosenstein brothers to fill in when we needed extra players. There was only one drawback: Mrs. Rosenstein was the grouchiest of any of my friends' parents and if you caught her on a bad day (actually I don't think I ever saw her on a good day) she could be scary—Roald Dahl–level scary.

Fortunately she usually ignored us, but I still have memories of her losing her temper and screaming at her sons or even at us as if we were her sons. What I remember best, though, was the time she came out to the driveway to interrupt a late afternoon two-on-two game by announcing, "Jeremy and Michael, go inside right now and wash up for dinner." Then she turned to me and Jim Cohn: "We are about to eat," and here she almost seemed to smile for a moment, "and you boys are invited . . . to leave."

At the time it struck me as a kind of perverse and malicious act—inviting someone to stay and then turning and inviting someone else to leave—but as I grow older I've slowly come to understand its usefulness. I've even come to recognize that as a writer I've been inviting certain people to leave for some time now. Actually I'm not sure I would have noticed if others hadn't pointed it out to me. Over the past ten years or so I've published a number of autobiographical essays about teaching in academic journals. Most of these pieces are case studies of my own classroom in which, along the way, I confess to certain quirks, idiosyncrasies, and failures as a teacher of writing. The confessions usually focus on my inability to live up to what I take to be the profession's agreed-upon standards of honesty, consistency, fairness, and integrity. For instance,

1

I might admit to being tempted to give students lower grades than they deserve because they argue with me about previous grades, support political positions that I find personally offensive, or look, dress, and act like fraternity types.

Ha ha!

Now these confessions are not non sequiturs; at least they are not meant to be. I introduce them as part of a scholarly investigation of a teaching problem. For instance, I might be examining resistance in the classroom or the difficulty of objective grading or gender issues in teacher-student relationships and I will illustrate these issues by talking about my own neurotic, ill-tempered behavior. I've always felt these personal confessions serve as the kind of specific, concrete examples we always ask for in our students' own writing. I've hoped that these personal examples help establish me as a credible and sympathetic narrator. And I've come to realize that the self-reflective material in my essays is what distinguishes them from the majority of scholarly academic articles; it may even be the primary reason I'm able to get my stuff published.

But, as I found out lately, it is also what has made some of my colleagues in composition dislike my work. Though most of the responses I've received are positive and generous, a significant percentage are from people who are enormously put out and put off by the form and content of personal scholarship. Several years ago I submitted a piece to a scholarly journal on the difficulties I often have when I teach writing to aggressive adolescent males: while one outside reader praised it for the clarity and honesty of the voice, the other rejected it saying, "I not only hate this article; I also hate this author." And so I've had reason to ask myself this: by including personal material in a scholarly piece of writing, who will I invite in and who will I invite out?

I'd like to think I'm inviting in smart, secure, good-natured readers and excluding pompous, pedantic, humorless ones but, of course, that's more than a little self-serving. From the responses I have received to my writing, I now know that there are a significant number of readers out there who just think that confessional writing and personal anecdotes have no place in academic writing. Or maybe they just aren't interested in why my mother had to ask that sadistic clown to leave my fifth birthday party, why my daughter's friend's mother blacked out some of the words in her copy of *Snow White,* or why I couldn't believe it when my grandmother said "*Again* with the long-distance calls?" as I phoned my brother to tell him that our mother had survived the surgery. (I know you're probably siding with my critics, but you'll have to take my word for it: these anecdotes had something to do with what I was saying about teaching.)

What strikes me as odd is not the preference for or against the use of personal material in academic writing; it's the extent and passion of that preference. Now I'm trying not to take this distaste for personal writing personally: after all, academics who cite charts and graphs have complete disdain for academics who cite Lacan or Foucault who have complete disdain for academics who fail to cite anyone at all. But while there is more than enough academic contempt to go around for any and all prose styles, it is the autobiographical essay that has become the shibboleth in the contemporary English department.

Some of this has to do with disagreements in the culture at large. Like the incestuous material in Kathyrn Harrison's memoir *The Kiss*, Kenneth Starr's report on Lewinsky and Clinton, or an episode of *The Jerry Springer Show*, autobiographical essays function in the academy as litmus tests of our attitudes about confession, privacy, and propriety. Whether we are debating the appropriateness of including autobiographical writing in our own scholarship or of asking our students to write personal narratives in our composition courses, the sides are clearly drawn. Those opposed to autobiographical writing usually argue—in sophisticated prose that takes a great deal of rigor and learning to decode—that personal writing is just not sufficiently sophisticated or rigorous or learned or theorized to be of much scholarly value; those in favor tend to tell personal stories about our own experience as teachers and as writers.

Like this one. For years—in high school, college, graduate school—I wrote only traditional academic discourse. I never told a story, revealed a private thought, doubt, or anxiety, or used highly colloquial language. My first publications—a heavily theoretical piece using French feminist theory to interpret court proceedings of women accused of witchcraft in seventeenth-century Boston and a quantitative study of writing and computers with charts and graphs and claims of interrated reliability—were strikingly academic and apersonal. I had written myself so completely out of those texts that producing them was a kind of out-of-body experience: by publishing academic essays, I had finally gained entry into an exclusive club. The price, though, was high: I had invited myself to leave.

It wasn't until I began to describe my own teaching experience, particularly my own teaching fears and failures, that I began to feel confident about and connected to my own writing—and I began to receive very positive support and very angry criticism. That my entry into my own writing should be the occasion of some readers' exit seems a strange irony. But maybe, given our many cultural, familial, and temperamental differences, this is inevitable. A few years ago I had a telling exchange with a composition scholar whose work on the politics and social constructedness of language I respect but don't particularly identify with or even fully understand. She feels the same way about my work, I imagine. She said something like, "I think that asking students to write personally is trolling for intimacy. And in my family trolling for intimacy was considered rude." To which I responded, "In my family *not* trolling for intimacy was considered rude."

That's why I am slowly giving up the fantasy that I will be loved by every reader and growing comfortable, even pleased, to be writing instead for a somewhat exclusive audience. In fact, maybe that is what I really wanted to accomplish by introducing personal material into scholarly writing in the first place. I used to complain to Tom Newkirk, a friend and colleague, about the negative reaction I received to some of my personal pieces, to which Tom responded, "I don't get it: you try so hard to be provocative and then get upset when readers are provoked."

The scary thing is that my academic confessions are actually fairly innocuous. I confess that I sometimes don't prepare for class or sometimes dislike students for no fair reason. In an essay that appears as a chapter in this book, I reveal, among other things, that I have certain biases against certain aggressive, baseball cap-wearing, male students. I reveal some aspects of my bias, exaggerate other aspects of it, conceal still other aspects. I know it is provocative to admit these biases, and yet I am always shocked when some readers are shocked.

Maybe more than shocked, I get scared. I immediately think, "Those trivial confessions shocked you? You don't know the half of it." Like Dimmesdale in *The Scarlet Letter,* I have offered relatively safe confessions that only mask my real sins. I have had thoughts about my students that are much more selfish, petty, erotic, neurotic, venal, and unevolved than any I've ever explored in print. But the fact that some readers are so easily put off or scandalized is strangely liberating. I know now that I'll probably never reach those readers and so I feel free not even to try.

In fact, I'm afraid that the criticism that I've been too confessional and too digressive for some academic readers has pushed me to confess and digress much more. Maybe it's that "imp of the perverse" that Poe described, that inner being that refuses to behave even or especially when someone demands propriety and good manners. I now find myself trying to write academic essays that are less conventionally academic and that move closer to memoir and creative nonfiction.

Of course, I know that I'm not all that unusual in my desire to experiment with hybrid forms of academic writing—there have for years now been numerous conference panels and journal articles that examine personal voice in academic discourse, creative nonfiction in composition—but I also know that many comp scholars still find these experiments transgressive or tiresome. A friend of mine who had assigned a chapter of my first book in a graduate seminar sent me her students' one-page reading responses. Most were positive but the negative ones were angry. And, in each case, that anger was based on my introduction of personal material. One student cited this anecdote from the book as especially irritating:

> In perhaps my worst moments I try to divide and conquer, to complain to the "good" students about the "bad" ones. It is, of course, a pathetic strategy: "I know that some of you are working really hard and I'm really pleased with your work. Unfortunately, though, for a class of this sort of work, everyone needs to make an effort and there are people in here who are not contributing anything." I wonder where I learned to teach like that? . . . [M]aybe I learned it from Pogo, the clown my parents hired to entertain at my fifth birthday party. According to family legend, as soon as he started to perform, I burst into tears, yelling, "I'm scared; I want him to leave." Pogo was upset, then embarrassed and hurt, and finally very angry. And so as he left the party he went over to the other kids and asked: "You liked the show, didn't you? And you wanted to see more of it. But now you can't and it's all because of Laddy. Don't you think Laddy is a little crybaby. (Tobin 1993, 78)

Ironically, that was the one of same sections singled out for praise by another reader who liked the book *because* I used my own personal experiences to illustrate the pleasures and pains of teaching: "I was especially struck by the clown story. Based on your references and my calculations, I'm figuring that event took place sometime in the early '60s or late '50s in the Chicago area, right? Are you aware that John Wayne Gacy, the mass murderer, worked as a clown in the Chicago area during that time under the name "Pogo"? Considering the unlikely odds that there were two Pogos entertaining at kids' parties and his crazy behavior, I'd say that there's no question that that clown was Gacy." Though I recounted the event as accurately as possible, the one detail I had invented—or thought I had invented—was the clown's name. I still have my doubts about whether that clown could have been Gacy (as best as I can determine, he made most of his clown appearances in the late '60s and early '70s, so unless it was not my fifth but my *fifteenth* birthday party, it probably was a different sadistic clown). Still, if this reader's hypothesis is right, I demonstrated precociously good judgment by identifying the mass murderer at my birthday party—and inviting *him* to leave.

See, that's one more reason for the inclusion of personal voice and storytelling in academic writing: it often leads to personal response and even better storytelling in return. At this point in my life and career, especially now that this issue has become so politicized, I can't imagine going back to conventional, apersonal academic discourse. Yet I also can't imagine critics of personal writing completely warming up to my style either. That's why I originally was tempted to follow Evelyn Rosenstein's lead and start this book with this warning label: "I'm about to write in a personal way about issues that come up for me when I read and respond to student writing; to examine those issues, I plan to talk about my experience as a patient in psychotherapy, as the son of a psychoanalyst, as a composition scholar in a department of literary theorists and cultural critics. If you are bored, bugged, or offended by personal narrative, confessional writing, or relentless self-study, you are invited . . . to leave." But that, too, was just that "imp of the perverse" speaking and doesn't reflect the contents or the spirit of this book. I'll confess that there are times when I think that the various camps of composition studies have grown so far apart that we just need to acknowledge our irreconcilable differences and go our separate ways. But I recognize those as times when I've let my frustration and defensiveness overwhelm my better judgment. In fact, what I'm arguing for in this book is not narrowness, exclusivity, and specialized languages but rather the inclusion of more dialogue, diversity, and hybridity in student writing and in our own scholarship.

So let me try again. I know that the issues I address in this book can be productively explored in all sorts of ways, including conventional academic scholarship. I also know that the essays I offer in this book, essays that seek to combine personal narrative and self-reflection with scholarly analysis, are not everyone's cup of tea. And so I'll certainly understand it if you decide that you've already read far enough to know this book will just get on your nerves and that you'd rather pass it along to that weird colleague of yours who goes in for this sort of thing. But, if you think you can stand it, I really would rather you stayed.

Introduction
The Elephant in the Classroom

Nerds Night Out

I remember that Libby was at the dinner, since she was the one person I knew before that night, and I know that Libby brought her friend Jean, since Jean was the one who got us started on the whole thing. I'm pretty sure that there were six of us altogether sitting around a big table at a small Thai restaurant but I can't remember now whether we were in Saint Louis or Milwaukee or Cincinnati. Since no one at the dinner knew everyone else—we each had brought a friend who had brought a friend—we had nothing in common except we were all in town to attend a conference for writing teachers. I remember we began talking about composition scholarship and teaching, which quickly deteriorated into griping about English department politics, which deteriorated further into griping about our least favorite students and then, finally, into what we each would describe as our "essay from hell."

Someone said that *her* worst nightmare of a student essay was one that she knew but couldn't prove was plagiarized; another said that she most dreaded the trite, clichéd essay about the tragic death of a relative or friend; a third complained about essays that went on and on about topics so vapid and trivial that he began *hoping* for a tragic death. Finally, Jean jumped in to say that, as a matter of fact, she had received her "essay from hell" just a few days before leaving for the conference. It was by a student whose politics, toward women in particular, offended her so much that she could barely finish reading to the last page. She told us that this student, who was living at home and commuting to classes, complained in his essay about his problems adjusting to college, which he mostly blamed on his mother for failing to have his laundry

7

done and his meals ready; as a result of her "slacking off," he wrote, he did not always look his best and once even had been late for an *important* party.

That a student would feel this way, let alone submit an essay confessing to feeling this way, seemed so mystifying and outrageous to all of us that we ended up talking about it for the rest of the dinner, the dessert, and the walk back to the hotel. After discussing the essay for another fifteen minutes in the lobby, we decided to continue our conversation in the hotel bar. Jean, though, said that she couldn't join us: she still had ten more essays to grade by Monday. "You don't have the essay that we've been talking about with you, do you?" someone asked. To our amazement and (okay, I'll admit it) near-exhilaration, she said that she did and that she would bring it down for us to read. The rest of us, proving that our nerdiness knew no bounds, spent the next five minutes gathered around the hotel's elevators excitedly anticipating Jean's return and the next two and a half hours in the hotel bar, nursing our beers and diet cokes, generating alternate interpretations of Jean's "essay from hell."

Someone in the group commented on how the writer's diatribe about his mother was just an uncensored version of commonly held misogynist notions about work, leisure, and domesticity. Someone else suggested the piece was clearly meant to be ironic and humorous. A third person thought the essay's author was struggling with his own sexual identity and that he was performing an exaggerated macho role in his relationship with his mother in an effort to cover up (from the reader *and* from himself) his latent desire for the certain male classmate (the quarterback of the university's football team) that he kept referring to in such glowing terms throughout the piece. I think it was at that point that (okay, I'll admit this, too) I suggested that the writer introduced the tension with the quarterback in an effort to cover up (from the reader *and* from himself) his latent desire for his mother and that the whole piece was really about unresolved Oedipal feelings.

I suspect some of this freewheeling discussion made Jean anxious—she kept bringing us back to important contextual information about the student's other essays, about his attitude and aptitude, about his responses or lack of responses in class and conference, about the anxiety she felt about having to respond to what he'd written—but the rest of us were having a blast. Free from the requirement to write a response to the essay or give it a grade or interact with its author, we felt free to play with the text, to speculate, to pursue personal associations and possible intertextual references, and to view the essay's gaps and inconsistencies as opportunities to draw on the approaches and theories—feminist, psychoanalytic, queer, cultural, reader-response—that informed our readings of other literary and cultural texts.

It all seemed so simple: bring together a group of writing teachers; distribute a provocative student essay; and ask them to read it with the same sort of creativity, effort, playfulness, and sense of collaboration that they would bring to their reading of, say, a poem, a short story, or an episode of *The Sopranos*. It all seemed so simple that night and early morning in the hotel, but returning home, I discovered that it wasn't all that easy to get such a group together, nor was it easy to undo habits learned during all those years of reading to find errors, reading to determine a grade, reading to get done with an unpleasant chore.

Squashing Bugs with Professor von X

It is after midnight on a winter night in November 1977. I am hunched over my desk, reading a student essay line by line, red pen in hand. The essay was written by a high school junior. It is on the same topic as the last three I have read and the same topic as the next twenty-one I still have to read: the symbolism of the river in *Huck Finn*. I have promised the students that I would return these essays to them tomorrow. I had meant to read them weeks ago but every time I took them out of my briefcase and scanned one, my heart would sink. They all seem dull, superficial; the writers all seem disinterested, detached.

I read each one the way I remember my father reading a bill in a restaurant—with a frown, searching for errors. I read as if I were Professor von X, the heavily built, small-eyed, red-faced scholar Virginia Woolf imagined she would have observed if women were allowed in the Oxbridge library, the one, Woolf wrote, who "was labouring under some emotion that made him jab his pen on the paper as if he were killing some noxious insect as he wrote, but even when he killed it that did not satisfy him; he must go on killing it; and even so, some cause for anger and irritation remained" (Woolf 1929, 31). Feeling compelled to write all these narrow columns of red ink in the margins on each essay is both a cause and a symptom of my irritation. I am reading each one against a mental template I have constructed—content, style, length, correctness. I allow room for originality but only within very narrow parameters—that is, I look for a clear thesis, persuasive evidence, a logical system of organization, clear transitions, a clear and relatively graceful style, and, of course, correctness. To go through this checklist, mark the errors and deviations, write out the "correct" answers in the margins, and then write a lengthy comment justifying the grade takes a great deal of time. I find this work absolutely exhausting and (I know how melodramatic I sound here) almost physically painful.

My frustration with these essays is not entirely unjustified. The papers read, not surprisingly, as if they have been written at the very last minute. I imagine the students putting off this assignment for months, ignoring the due date, thinking it would never arrive. I imagine them the night before the due date, at one in the morning, pleading, "Please God, just let me get through this one paper one more time and I'll never, ever, put off an assignment till so late again." Why, I think, am I stuck with such poorly prepared and poorly motivated students? Why haven't their teachers in junior high taught them how to write? And then, like the Charlie Kaufman character that Nicolas Cage plays in *Adaptation,* I decide I need to reward myself with a break to get me through the next five- or ten-minute interval of work.

[margin note: Identify]

A few hours later: I have now graded fifteen of the twenty-five essays. I find myself counting the graded essays again and again, hoping that I have graded more than I have. But each time the count comes out the same or, to my horror, I discover two essays paper-clipped together one of which I have not yet graded. I start to copy lines of response from the margins of other essays. It is now three in the morning and I still have five more essays to go. "Please God," I say, "just let me get through these last five essays and I'll never put off reading student essays till so late again."

[margin note: Same as students]

Everything Is a Text But *This* Is a Student Essay

When I started grad school in the mid '70s, I believed (along with almost everyone around me) that any text had a stable meaning that could be identified by intelligent readers willing to work hard enough to find it. But by the time I finished my doctorate, in the early '90s, I believed (again along with almost everyone around me) that all texts were unstable and indeterminate and that every reading was a rewriting that reflected a reader's own subjective position. Of course, I didn't come to any of this on my own. I had read the usual suspects: Iser, Derrida, Cixous, Kristeva, Said, Gilbert and Gubar, Jameson. I was hugely influenced by Roland Barthes' claim that it didn't matter if his reading of Balzac was accurate since, he confidently claimed, he was more interesting than Balzac, just as I was struck by Stanley Fish's story about telling his grad students that "what they saw on the blackboard was a religious poem of the kind they had been studying" (Fish 1980, 323) and then watching them discover all sorts of hidden meaning, connections, and intertextual associations in what actually was a list of the authors they were to read for the next class.

[margin note: critics, theories]

Still, for some reason, while my theories of literacy, textuality, and interpretation had undergone radical revision, while I had in fact come to believe that no text has a fixed or inherent meaning, my practice of reading student writing had not kept pace. As readers of any text *besides* those written by students, I was more than ready to accept relativism, postmodernism, multiplicity; but give me a batch of student essays to grade and I reverted to Prof von X and my old-fashioned methods.

[margin note: Interesting – we DO resort to this]

What finally changed my approach was not reading cutting-edge critical theory but rather observing innovative composition practice. In the mid '80s, after many years of experience as a high school teacher, an adjunct writing instructor, and a writing center director, I decided to go back to grad school as a doctoral student in comp/rhet. The first course I took, Writing for Teachers, was taught by Don Murray, the author of some of the most radical and practical works of the writing process movement. In our weekly one-to-one conferences, Don would read my writing in a very different way from how I was reading my students' work: while I sat across from him in his basement home office, he would read my essay very quickly, without a pen in his hand, and then ask me questions that, amazingly, suggested that he was enjoying himself, that he was willing and even eager to be instructed by what I had to say, and that he felt my writing could be interpreted in all sorts of ways. Nor was Don alone in this approach: arguments for generous, creative reading of student work are evident in almost all of the important composition scholarship of the late '70s and early '80s, including the work of Mina Shaugnessey, Peter Elbow, Ken Macrorie, David Bartholomae, and Nancy Sommers.

As a direct result of those powerful and influential models, I modified almost all of my teaching methods. From the moment I started reading drafts for potential rather than for assessment, my relationship to my students and my sense of myself as a writing teacher changed in fundamental and exhilarating ways. But like every other Brave New World experience, there was bound to come a moment when things stopped seeming quite so brave or quite so new. For me, that moment came when I had to admit that in spite of how much I was enjoying the different classroom relationships I had established, I still did not particularly like reading student writing. Of course, I could always blame my students for bringing so little energy, intelligence, and creativity to their essays, for holding back so much of themselves as writers, but I couldn't quite shake the notion that I was still looking too much for error and still working too hard to keep out my own personal associations. When I examined my way of reading against the standard described here by the rhetorician Robert Scholes (1989), I realized that my students weren't the only ones who were holding back:

> We should, in fact, read so as to get the most out of each experience of reading. If a book or a story or any other text is like a little life, and if our reading actually uses up precious time in that other story we think of as our lives, then we should make the most of the reading just as we should make the most of our lives. Reading reminds us that every text ends with a blank page and that what we get from every text is precisely balanced by

what we give. Our skill, our learning, and our commitment to the text will determine, for each of us, the kind of reading experience that text provides. Learning to read books—or pictures, or films—is not just a matter of acquiring information from text, it is a matter of learning to read and write the texts of our lives. (19)

I was forced to recognize that there remained a significant gap between the engaged way I read a book or a story and the relatively detached way I continued to read student writing. In part, this gap was understandable: a student essay is not a book or a story, and reading to be amused or informed is not the same as reading to provide instruction or assessment. Still, if what "we get from every text is precisely balanced by what we give," if every text is interesting to the extent to which we bring to it our attention, energy, and creativity, then frustration with a student essay is largely self-fulfilling.

What I needed, what I thought the field needed, was a more sophisticated and nuanced understanding of our role as readers of student writing. Toward that end, I published an essay in the early '90s in which I suggested, "We need a theory of reading that takes into account the 'intertextual' nature of our work; that is, a theory that acknowledges that we cannot read any student essay without unconsciously and simultaneously reading a number of other texts as well. Finally, we need a theory that allows us to recognize our own limitations" (Tobin 1991, 337). When I called for someone to take on such a project, I had no idea that I was assigning it to myself. Yet even when I tried to move on to what I thought were new and different topics—the effect of gender in the writing class, the role of the Internet in the acquisition of literacy skills, the rise of cultural criticism and the fall of the literary canon in departments of English, the causes of boredom and burnout in writing teachers—I found that I was always still striving to identify the role and nature of reading in the teaching of writing.

Why Write About Reading?

I think I keep coming back to reading because it is the single most important job we have as writing teachers. Though we tend to focus mostly on what we do as writing teachers *before* a course begins (choosing texts and topics) and what we do *after* it ends (assessment), I am suggesting in this book that what we do *during* a course (reading and responding to student writing in process) is what counts most. Just as the three keys to choosing real estate are "location, location, location," the three most important jobs of the writing teacher are reading (student essays), reading (student writers), and reading (ourselves as teachers). Or to put it another way: reading student texts; reading the context in which student writing occurs; and reading the unstated, usually unexamined subtext that shapes our readings, interpretations, and assessments. Reading a student essay is an enormously complicated and multidimensional task that involves reading the words on the page; reading the words we wish were on the page; reading the words we think the student wishes were on the page; reading the affect, temperament, ability, and potential of the student who wrote the words; reading our own emotional reaction to that student and that text; reading our relationships to our colleagues, mentors, and campus administrators; and so on.

Fortunately, the skills required for this sort of reading are not entirely new to us. In fact, as readers of novels, newspapers, articles in academic journals, movies, and advertisements, we have become experienced experts. But, as opposed to almost all of our "real world" reading material (say, novels, newspapers, articles in academic journals, movies, and advertisements), we are as writing teachers often reading works that are in progress, that were written by novice and occasionally unmotivated authors, and that grew in some way out of an assignment we gave and will grow eventually into an assessment we will give. For all of these reasons, reading and responding to student writing is particularly fraught and complex.

One way to think about that complexity would be to say that a productive reading of a student-authored text requires a nuanced reading of context. But even that would not fully get at the difficulty, because what I am suggesting in this book is that there is no clear line between text and context, reading and writing. This, of course, is also not a new or unfamiliar concept to most of us in English studies. We know the arguments against the determinacy of meaning in texts, against validity and objectivity in interpretation, against fixed notions of truth, authenticity, and honesty. And that knowledge has had a profound impact on the way we craft writing assignments (for example, it helps to explain the backlash against the idea of a stable author or an authentic voice) and on the readings we assign in first-year writing courses (for example, the increased emphasis on cultural studies and popular culture).

In this book, though, I focus primarily on what happens after course design and before response and assessment. My interest is in how we construct and conduct ourselves as readers of student writing. I've organized the book into three main sections: Reading Student Writing; Reading Ourselves as Writing Teachers; and Reading the Teaching of Writing. In the first section, I look carefully at the problems of reading and interpreting student writing by focusing on examples of student writing that teachers generally find particularly problematic: texts about cultural difference; texts about trauma and loss; texts that threaten to pull us into the role of therapist; and texts that either rehearse of resist stereotypes about gender. "How Many Writing Teachers Does

It Take to Read a Student Essay?" lays out the framework for the entire book by offering multiple, theoretically informed readings of a single student essay about cultural differences and stereotypes. What I hope I demonstrate is that the more time we spend on a student essay, the more teachers and scholars we invite to offer readings, the richer the text begins to appear and the more we come to appreciate what initially might seem superficial or naïve or even offensive in a student essay. In "Reading and Writing About Death, Disease, and Dysfunction, or How I Spend My Summer Vacations," I suggest that one way to explain the nature and prevalence of student writing about trauma and loss is to pay more attention to our own experience as adolescents and student writers. In "Replacing the Carrot with the Couch: Reading Pyschotherapeutically," I argue that writing instruction and psychotherapy have much in common and that in order to read student writing intelligently, we need to become much more systematic about self-study and self-presentation. In the final chapter in this section, "Car Wrecks, Baseball Caps, and Man-to-Man Defense: The Personal Narratives of Adolescent Males," I look at gender as a key factor in our interpretation of students and their writing.

In the second section, Reading Ourselves as Writing Teachers, I look even more explicitly at the ways that a teacher's own values, biases, assumptions, and unconscious associations shape readings of student writing. In "Fear and Loathing of Fear and Loathing," I suggest that our own ambivalence about our students' expression of strong emotions often leads us to read and respond to them in inconsistent and reductive ways. In "Referring Ourselves to the Counseling Center: Confronting Boredom and Burnout in the Teaching of Writing," I explore how our boredom and burnout may be the cause rather than the effect of our frustration with student writing. In the last chapter in this section, "Teaching with a Fake ID," I argue that we need to construct ourselves as readers of student writing in much broader and more realistic ways.

The final section, Reading the Teaching of Writing, makes the case that we cannot separate our interpretation and assessment of student writing from our position in and attitudes toward the field. "Reading Composition's Misplaced Anxieties About Personal Writing" focuses on how our field's discomfort with personal writing has misled us as readers of students and their work. In "What We're Walling In, What We're Walling Out: Reading (and Rewriting) Our Own Bad Assignments," I make the case that when we read a trite essay about a roommate problem or a boring research paper about whales or a simplistic argument about abortion, we are generally reading our own bad assignments funneled back to us as text. I then argue that we need more often to assign and read student writing through the lens of creative nonfiction. "Reading Our Classrooms, Writing Our Selves," the final chapter, suggests that part of our problem in reading student essays in imaginative ways is that many of us find ourselves in English departments that refuse to treat students, student writing, or pedagogy as texts or topics worthy of serious study. In order to read a student text productively, we also need to read the subtext and context productively. That is, we need to learn to read our students, our classrooms, and ourselves.

Taken together, these personal essays attempt to make a case for new theories, attitudes, and methods in the way we read and respond to student writing. And yet my suggestions are more *what if* than *how to*. My guess is that some of these suggestions—for example, giving ourselves permission to read rough drafts with less focus and precision in order to explore our own unconscious associations—may initially seem counterintuitive, while others—such as reading each student's text against our reading of the student writer as text and our reading of the classroom as context—may seem overly ambitious given the time constraints we all face as teachers. My hope, though, is that these essays will stir things up and will generate questions, counterproposals, and other personal narratives about how interesting and difficult it can be to read a student essay.

Trying Not to Shoot or Even Think About an Elephant

What we need is to write roles for ourselves as readers of student writing that are more flexible, nuanced, and realistic. After years of struggling to compose an effective teaching persona, I've come to believe that our hypervigilance about objectivity, fairness, and professionalism not only makes our job more frustrating and less satisfying but also makes us less effective as writing teachers. I'm not suggesting that we should *strive* to be unfair and unprofessional (we can do *that* without trying); I'm just suggesting that we've been too timid, too cautious, and, in some ways, too hard on ourselves. To write a more effective role for ourselves would require, for one thing, that we stop thinking so much about what we think we're *supposed* to do, what we think our students and colleagues *expect* us to do, and begin thinking and talking more about the issues that actually make the job of reading student writing so interesting and rewarding but also so complicated and stressful.

I've tried in this book to write about the elephants in the room, that is, the issues we usually avoid, such as what happens when reading student writing leaves us bored and burned out, pulls us out of our role as teacher and into the role of therapist, or for some reason makes us feel like a fake or a fraud. I know I run a risk by stretching this metaphor so thin, but there is one elephant that it is particularly productive to think about here—the one that Orwell so famously and unhappily shot in his canonical personal essay. Orwell says he shot that elephant knowing that it was a mistake and that it went against his better judgment simply because it was expected of him; long before the episode, he had recognized the evils that imperialism imposed on colonial subjects; what he finally realized in shooting the elephant was that the system also dehumanized, disempowered, and severely constrained the imperialist tyrant as well.

I know, of course, that any attempt to compare traditional writing instruction to British imperialism trivializes the abuses of imperialism and insults traditional teachers, but I'm convinced that there is something important we can learn from Orwell's narrative about reading student writing. And so with profuse apologies for taking such profane license, I want to confess that I think Orwell's essay speaks in some way to the overly cautious and uncreative roles we have written for ourselves as readers of student writing. Orwell writes that his whole life at that time was "one long struggle not to be laughed at" (1936, 573). That a composition instructor, like a subdivisional police officer, might be motivated primarily by a fear of embarrassment and of losing control is not surprising, but as Orwell's disastrous shooting of that elephant reminds us, there are far worse fates than occasionally looking like a fool.

1

How Many Writing Teachers Does It Take to Read a Student Essay?

The first time I read "The Googu Manifesto" was during an in-class workshop. Sandeep had volunteered to discuss his essay and had brought copies so that we could all look on while he read the piece aloud. By the time he was halfway though, I started to panic. Generally I feel pretty confident about responding on the fly to student writing, but listening to "The Googu Manifesto," I felt disoriented and confused. Was Sandeep's essay as offensive as it seemed, or was I somehow missing the point? Was it meant to be funny? And, since the essay's conclusion seemed to come completely out of left field, should I suggest that he cut it and focus on just one, main idea? Or should I just ask him to choose a new topic altogether?

Sandeep had produced his essay in response to an assignment that probably felt disorienting and confusing to many of my students:

> Write an informative and entertaining human-interest story. Your story could be about a current craze, fad, countercultural phenomena, subculture scene or group, quirky local character. You will need to observe your subject(s) firsthand, conduct interviews, gather relevant information. In order to put your subject(s) in context, you may also need to do some research in the library and on the Internet.

I then suggested that they look for models for the sort of short feature pieces that I wanted in our textbook, *Dressing for Dinner in the Naked City*. A collection of middle columns from the *Wall Street Journal, Dressing for Dinner* includes well-written and carefully researched human-interest pieces on quirky topics: people who collect PEZ dispensers; a NY–style hair salon in Dallas that won't do Big Hair; a company that organizes proms for correspondence schools; a law firm in southern California that represents animals charged with

17

crimes; a maggot-fishing competition that takes place in polluted, industrial canals.

When Sandeep volunteered to read, we had already workshopped pieces on the etiquette of raves; a "night in the life" of a cab driver who works for a Haitian American taxicab company; and a profile of the woman who invented "The Chocolate Orgasm," a recent winner of *Boston Magazine's* "best local dessert." Though I think we all still had slightly different ideas about the conventions and parameters of the human-interest story, we all seemed in agreement that Sandeep's piece was something else altogether. But exactly what that thing was, I couldn't say. Here's the piece:

"The Googu Manifesto"
Arlington, Texas

Most people are not familiar with the Indian community. Most Indians came to America just within the past ten to twenty years. Also most of them are from the state in India called Gutrat. They are known as Gutraty people and are more prevalent in Texas then any other regional peoples of India. But as most of the Indians are Gutraty, they have a very unfavorable stereotype. They are all considered cheap and have received the nickname of "gugoo." The amusing fact of this matter is most gutraty people don't find this offensive at all, and admit it. Not that it is a derogatory term as "Nigger" is and has been for African-Americans. But that it is just a joke that seems to be carried out by most Indians for comic relief. Even though it does have some backing.

Gugoo's are so cheap that I could go on and list it forever. But it is much better explained, for gugoo's seem to want to get everything for free. For instance when they go to Taco Bell they never leave without having about a bag full of taco bell hot sauce packets that they use so they don't have to buy hot sauce. When they are at any other restaurant they will make sure that the whole family has as many sugar packets they can fit in their pockets. Some will have entire meals at grocery stores that give away free samples of food. It is not that they do not have money to live with, but that being cheap is just a way of life even for the wealthy. They will take anything that is free, no matter what it is, if they can use it or not. Their are even "your momma so googu" jokes like "you mamma so googu she asked for a discount at the dollar store," and many others that seem to take cheapness to an extreme. But the proceeding is just the parents, the new generation googu's are even worse. They will take stuff just to take it. Like taking the pepper and cheese shakers at pizza places, even hot sauce bowls at Mexican restraunts. Or one time our school was at a Math and Science competition at a big complex. Well the organisers of the contest had free pizza and cokes for everyone, everyone supposed to just take one drink. But the googu's all scrambled for the cokes and filled their bags with them. They even took a useless contraption called a "tweejet," that was used for one of the questions in the competition. Then to top it of another googu took the little plastic contraption that had the name of our school. These kind of outlandish actions cause googu's to live up to their reputation.

Being gugoo is not only a term for Gutraties, but a state of being. Many atimes my friend Raj and I have ventured out into the world trying to see how googu we could be. For being googu is trying to get everything for free or at a discount. For instance Raj and I will head out for a day at the mall, but we are not out to buy anything, but get stuff for free. Since we are trying to achieve a state of googuness we must not buying anything, just try to get food and drinks for free. This is not a very easy task but with very tactful thinking it can be achieved. The first thing we do when we are thirsty is go straight to Whataburger (A hamburger chain in Texas). Due to the fact that Whataburger has a promotion that it sponsors with the Texas Rangers which gives away free drinks for dot race tickets. Now a dot race ticket can be either red, yellow, or green, and they are given out during Rangers games. The rules are if your color wins during the dot race which is run during the 7th inning you win a free 16oz. Drink. Well due to our tactful googu impersonation we are able to sniff out the flaws in the tickets. They are supposed to be redeemed within five days after the game, but they have no dates on them. Plus all of the all year long look exactly the same. Thus no matter who wins one can use them during the season as long as the rangers are not on a road trip. Therefore we order just drinks and pay from them with the tickets. Then when we get hungry browsing the mall we must find some "connections" and get hooked up. So on any given day we might go to Baskin Robins were one of our friends Charles works. He in turn will give us free Ice cream so we are full and can go home. We have just completed a day of being googu because we received free food and drinks, and did not spend a penny.

One footnote that is also associated with googu's is their parents overprotection. Googu's are not usually allowed to go out later than 10:00 P.M., no matter how old they are. As long as they live with their parents. They cannot go on trips with their friends, and even go out with their friends until they are 18. They are not even allowed to have a girlfriend or boyfriend which is not allowed by most Indians but never allowed by googu's. The classification of googu's goes way beyond cheapness, but that is the one that can be exploited the most. For whenever there is a dull moment we (non googu's) bring up the other attributes of googu's.

What confused me most about The "Manifesto" was that I could not immediately or even finally locate the writer in relation to the issues he was raising. As Sandeep's teacher, I had information that should have helped reduce this confusion. I knew, for example, that when he read the piece aloud he pronounced *Googu* (which he sometimes spelled *gugoo*) not as *Goo-goo* but as *Goo-ja* and that he was using to term to refer to "people from Gutrat, which is, like, a region in India" (actually, I discovered later, the region he was referring to was not Gutrat, but Gujarat). I also was fairly certain, from his name and appearance, that Sandeep was Indian American, but it took me till the last sentence—till that parenthetical we *(non-googus)*—to be certain that his family was not from Gujarat.

But even with this information, I was still confused. It seemed clear that the author wanted us to laugh at the Googus, but was he also making some sort of serious point? And why did he include the information about the strictness of the Googus' parents? Of course, my first assumption was that all of the problems were in his writing and not in my reading. After all, we generally teach students that their writing ought to be clear, that they need to present enough description and exposition to make their analysis, interpretation, or argument understandable and effective. Our assumption is that if we have to work too hard as a reader, then the student has failed as a writer. (However, when we confront other resisting texts—an abstract poem, an artifact from another time or place, a complicated legal document—we assume that we need to educate ourselves in order to read it effectively.)

Before I could tell Sandeep to go back and make his essay clearer, more straightforward, less mysterious, I needed to know much more than I did about the context and background of this piece of writing; I also needed to know more about his own intentions. So, for starters, I asked the author what he was trying to accomplish in "The Googu Manifesto." "It's supposed to be funny; I mean, it *is* funny," he said, clearly surprised that there could be any question, "and it tells you what Googus are like." So, as far as Sandeep could tell, he had provided exactly what I'd asked for: a piece of writing that was both entertaining and informative.

The students in the workshop seemed nervous, presumably worried about the same issues that were worrying me. One of them spoke up tentatively: "Isn't this offensive to the," here she hesitated for a second, staring at the essay and apparently trying to figure out the correct pronunciation, "isn't this offensive to the Goojas?" Sandeep laughed. "No; not at all. I mean, they *understand*. You should hear what *they* say about us. This is *nothing* compared to what they say about us." Another student asked, also tentatively: "But wouldn't they be offended if they read this?" Sandeep shook his head. "It's meant to be funny; that's the point."

I was tempted to jump in and say something about how hurtful and dangerous ethnic humor can be, about how easy it is to connect jokes, for example, about Jewish stinginess to the propaganda and violence that eventually followed. But I worried about overreacting, about being too PC, about having invited a student to try a new form, to take risks, to educate me, and then to say, "This is offensive; this is inappropriate. I will not have this kind of talk in my classroom, young man." And I worried that maybe, as a Jew, I was too overidentified with those poor Googus and their thriftiness and overprotective parents to appreciate a harmless joke at their expense. With time running out, I said only that Sandeep's essay raised "complicated questions" that we would need to discuss in the next class.

Here were two of the complicated questions that I knew I needed to sort out:

- Just what *was* Sandeep's subject position or authorial stance? In other words, where was he located vis-à-vis the Gugoo question: an insider? an outsider? both? And did his subject position give him some sort of license to make those jokes?
- What was going on in that seemingly non sequitur conclusion about the Googus' parents? Was it a problem of focus, organization, transitions? Or was there a connection that I was missing?

In his weekly conference, which took place a day after the workshop, Sandeep still seemed frustrated when I asked him if he thought some readers, especially Googus, might be offended by his piece.

You really think some readers will be offended? Then I think I need to show the humor better. I don't want anyone who reads it to be appalled. The Googus *really* don't mind. Really. And, look, I tried to show that acting like a Googu isn't really a bad thing. I showed how I did it and how anyone can do it. [Here he shook his head and laughed.] But the thing is with the Googus, it's in *everything* they do. I mean that tweetjet they took; it was a useless piece of a useless contraption. There was just no point in taking it, but they still did. I'm not sure how the whole thing started.

It may be just an Arlington thing or just a Texas thing, but I don't think so, because I asked my friend in New Jersey and he said they have the same stereotype for Googus there. And a friend on the Internet in upstate New York said so, too. I don't think it started in India, though. I mean, I don't know all that much about India, but I've heard people say because India is just so different and too populated for a stereotype like this to exist. And besides there's no place in India to get free stuff.

But it may have *something* to do with India, because I've heard that in India the Googus usually have more money and more education than the Northern Indians—that's where my family is from—and the Southern Indians. But I think it has more to do with the way Googus act when they come to America. In my town they tried to separate themselves from all the other Indian students. They didn't even admit they were Indian; they said they were Googus, which was separate. They call themselves MFGs, which stands for Mother-Fucking Googus. They thought being Indian was so uncool. We all went through that phase, but they stick to it. Maybe we came up with the teasing about them being cheap to get back at them. But they don't mind. Actually I think all of the teasing goes back to something that happened our senior year. There were eight of us—four couples—and we decided to celebrate our graduation by going to Austin for a weekend. There were two northern Indians, a southern Indian, two Googus, two whites, and a Filipino. Everyone's parents said no at first, but after a while all the kids were able to go—except the Googus. And I think that is why we started talking all the time about them being Googus, 'cause that bothered me.

I was struck by how much Sandeep's comments in conference paralleled the structure of "The Googu Manifesto." Here, too, he started off marveling and laughing at the Googus' cheapness, blaming their reputation on their own outlandish behavior, and then concluding by expressing anger once again that they are controlled so much by their parents. "But, don't worry," Sandeep concluded, "my piece really isn't offensive. Ask Ravi. His family is from there."

Ravi was another student in our class. I was stunned to discover what seemed a remarkable coincidence—that another student in our fifteen-person seminar was from a Gujarati family. I was also surprised that Sandeep would have written about Googus in that way when he knew the essay would be workshopped by a Gujarati classmate who, as far as I could tell, seemed to be a good friend of his. I was also surprised by Ravi's response when I asked him how he felt about Sandeep's essay:

I never even heard the term until I met Sandeep and he said, "So you're a Googu?" and I said, "Well, yeah, I guess so," 'cause I sort of knew what he meant. It didn't bother me. Maybe if Sandeep wasn't Indian I'd think, "Hey, how do you know anything about us?" But it really didn't bother me coming from him. I don't think he thinks being from Gujarat is only a bad thing. It was weird listening to it in the workshop, in front of kids who aren't Indian, though. That bothered me much more than his saying it. But I got to admit that the weirdest thing was when he got to the part about the Taco Bell hot sauce: I thought, "Hey, I've got about twenty containers of that stuff back in my dorm room right now." So it made me think, "*Is* there something to this?"

The more I talked about this essay, the more interested I became in it and the more I wondered how other readers with different perspectives and areas of expertise would see it. For some time I had been thinking and arguing that we too often approach student writing with arrogance, assuming that we know how to read every piece on every subject in every genre. For some time I had been suggesting that the student essay seemed to be the only form of writing and only material artifact that we as English professors would or could not treat as a *text*. But for some other reasons (habit? a lack of time?), I continued to read student essays as if I could, without the assistance of collaboration, consultation, or research, quickly identify their meaning, deficits, and needs. What, I wondered, would I learn if I did the sort of research about Sandeep's essay that I do when I am studying other literary and cultural texts? What if I were to consult with experts on, say, postcolonial theory, Indian immigration in Texas, teenage teasing and humor?

And so, with Sandeep's consent, I decided to use his essay as a test case. I distributed "The Googu Manifesto" to scholars in postcolonial theory, American studies, anthropology, performance theory, and other fields that might be able to shed some light on the issues that Sandeep was raising. I included the following instructions: "Please read 'The Googu Manifesto' not as a teacher but as a scholar and as a reader. What takes your attention? What strikes you as significant? What can we learn from this piece of writing? What do we need to know or learn in order to read it effectively?"

Not surprisingly, most of the readers addressed the question of the writer's complex subject position. A scholar in African American studies focused primarily on the issue of license:

> I connect the term "googu" with the term "nigger" even though the writer argued that there is a clear distinction in the way these words are used. The whole tone is reminiscent in some ways of racial issues about Af Am; that's why I connect the teasing between the writer's subgroup and the Googus—I had immediately thought of how it intersects with "the dozens," so I was not surprised when he said that the talk included Yo Mamma jokes. People outside a group do not have license to use certain terms—nigger, for example. That does not mean that some people outside the group won't use the term *without* license, but clearly that use carries a very different connotation than the term is intended to carry in this essay. In that respect, Googu is like Nigger. He feels that he can use it because, while not a Googu himself, he *is* Indian and therefore feels he has a license.

What interests me, the larger issue that strikes me, is why and how any minority—Jews, blacks, Indian Americans—reinvents derogatory terms for use in their own culture. The term of course takes on a very different meaning and has a specific and useful purpose coming out of a specific mouth from within that culture. In that reinventing the speaker resists and overturns the power of the racist language. But of course here the speaker uses two terms—Googu and Nigger—that both seem somewhat outside his immediate group. The point, I think, is that while not a Googu, he identifies himself as Indian and, while not African American, he identifies himself as a person of color, and so he believes that those identifications give him some license to use both terms. I'm not sure that *I* would give him license to use the word "nigger," even in this context, but I'd more likely to give it to *him* than, if he were, say, a white student from Stamford, Connecticut.

Reading "The Gugoo Manifesto" through the lens of the dozens is completely in synch with Sandeep's own claim that "maybe we came up with the teasing about them being cheap to get back at them," that the Gugoos' rejection of Indianness as "uncool" was an insult that had to be answered; that, in fact, the teasing was part of an ongoing rivalry and perhaps even intimacy between members of the group.

But what exactly *was* the group and was Sandeep inside or outside it? Another colleague, this one in American studies and culture, noted the confusion surrounding Sandeep's "insider status" and his ambiguous and ambivalent relationship to the Googus:

> One realm of interest for me comes out of scholarship done on "minstrel masking" in the nineteenth century, particularly the phenomenon that Eric Lott calls "love and theft." That is, Lott stresses both the affection and the cruelty of such performances, and stresses how they work in a fluid way to construct identity. For this professional reason, I would resist any attempt to "police" this student into shame about having "played a stereotype"—since in my professional head I think of this process of minstrel masking as quite complex. The last paragraph about parents is quite telling here, since it is the matter that most directly addresses assimilation, the topic stressed in the opening but never quite followed through on.

Almost all of the scholars and theorists who read this piece focused in some way on the tension between Sandeep's status as both insider and outsider and on the way he seemed to resist and disdain his own association with the Googus. A professor in Irish studies was most interested in the tension the writer seems to exhibit about possibly being mistaken for a Googu:

I am struck by the presence of absence, particularly the absence of self early in the essay. The writer is so defensive in the introduction. Read the personal pronouns. It is not until the reference to "our school" that the writer acknowledges something about *his* place in this narrative. I take it to be an essay about his ambivalence about his own identity. At that science fair he felt tremendous anxiety that to "the other," to the white Texans—to use a different cultural stereotype—he would be just another Indian or Googu. And so he is trying desperately to individuate himself. The ambivalence, though, is evident in his attempt to achieve a state of Googuness. He wants it both ways—to be part of an identifiable group and to individuate himself from that group at the same time. I see this ambivalence—this mix of anger or rage at "the other" and humiliation or disgust at the self—in much of the contemporary Irish fiction I am studying.

So was the writer making fun of the Googus because they were so like or so unlike other non-Googu Indians? I asked that question of a scholar who studies humor theory. He recommended, first, that I read Bergson and Freud on the topic of sadistic humor and then offered this comment:

What is most interesting about the confusion of the insider-outsider identity is that most humor and certainly most ethnic humor is about that very anxiety, that is, about differentiating yourself from a person or group who represents characteristics that are uncomfortably close to your own. People generally make ethnic jokes about groups that are most like rather than most unlike themselves.

An expert in performance theory also helped me sort out the writer's status as both insider and outsider:

The Googu essay made me think of an essay by Sue-Ellen Case titled "Toward a Butch-Femme Aesthetic." One of her arguments is that gay men as well as lesbians have been well aware of the stereotypes about gays and lesbians and that they have made it a practice to perform the stereotypes in exaggerated ways. She argues that "camp" was invented by gay and lesbian subcultures, as a strategy of resistance. They deliberately appropriated and parodied roles such as that of the "butch" and the "femme" in order to undermine those roles. I think the student is struggling to say something like that right from the first paragraph: "But that it is just a joke that seems to be carried out by most Indians for comic relief. Even though it does have some backing." Here, I think the student is falling back on a term like "comic relief" because he does not yet have a more critical language (about appropriation and parody) at his disposal. I read his reference to "trying to achieve a state of googuness" as also intentionally parodic.

Sandeep's decision to role-play Googuness also seemed crucial to this critical theorist:

> It's interesting here to look for "aporia" or "knitting points" or "uncanny moments" where the apparent coherence of a text breaks down. For me, the key phrase that strikes me as odd and problematic is "achieve a state of Googuness." It is ironic, mock serious. I suppose this effect is intentional. But what is the intent? Maybe to bring up an intertextual association with Hindi's or Buddhists' quests for high planes of consciousness: the Googus' mall escapades become a parody and repetition of the young Buddha's travels and of the ascetics who would eat little, and because they would never use money, would have to beg. Begging, of course, has other meanings in contemporary India that this text may also be referencing and parodying in the scene in which these middle-class, Indian American kids, who seem not very religious, are going around town, begging, living without dirtying their hands with money, and thereby achieving "a state of Googuness," a kind of mock-transcendence.

An anthropologist also picked up on this element of self-parody:

> It might make sense to look through a postcolonial lens at the way in which the author indulges in self-exoticism. The colonial condition is to see oneself through the colonizers' eyes as an exotic. The author here offers a not very sympathetic ethnography of himself and other Indian immigrants in Texas, making them strange, rather than familiar, as if they were an exotic tribe of humans.

By exaggerating the Googus' thriftiness, by making them so exotic as to become almost nonhuman, Sandeep had perhaps found a way to resist or parody my "human interest" assignment. At the same time, according to a novelist and creative writing teacher, it was this exaggeration that made "The Googu Manifesto" such a compelling read:

> The Googus are fascinating to me because they are like sci-fi characters— you know the sort who have only one characteristic. In this essay, the Googus exist on the planet solely for one purpose: to find free things. They are surface takers who will grab anything that is not nailed down. Other than *that*, they seem to have no *human motivation*—except, of course, in the last paragraph about their parents, which, for that reason, works against the rest of the portrait.

And, in fact, it was that last paragraph that most mystified the scholars I consulted. ("I'm still not sure why he brings up the parents' overprotectiveness at that point in the piece," wrote one. "In the final two sentences, does he mean that they exploit the cheapness stereotype when it suits them for their own amusement or that they exploit it to embarrass other Indians?" wrote another.) The most interesting explanation for this apparent non sequitur was offered by another anthropologist:

> I'm interested in the two different economies, the two different kinds of excitement—libidinal and literal—that seem to be at work in this paper: there is a socially sanctioned economy of (free) consumption, which produces a feeling of pleasure in the consumer, and, in the last paragraph, there is a repressed economy of sexual desire: the kids have to be home by ten and not be sexually active. The sexual thrill of the Googuing, I would argue, is present in the language used to describe the activity; this interpretation that Googuing is a sublimation or replacement for sex and intimacy is confirmed by the last paragraph, which appears as if it were an afterthought—I find when I interview informants that they often add something right at the end to make sure I get the point of what came before—but it is actually an attempt to explain the Googuing as resistance and sublimation.

This anthropologist then recommended that I pursue this point by looking at Keya Ganguly's essay "Migrant Identities: Personal Memory and Construction of Selfhood" (1992).

In fact, Ganguly's scholarship focuses uncannily on the very issues that Sandeep explores in his human-interest piece. First, Ganguly speaks to the confusion of the speaker's status and identification by asserting that the construction of a postcolonial identity is bound to be "articulated in multiple modalities" because (and here she is citing Homi Bhaba) "the question of identity is always posed uncertainly, tenebrously between shadow and substance" (46). Ganguly also speaks to the one-dimensional aspect of the Googus when she points out that while the ways in which Indian immigrants think of themselves as Indian are not stable and inherent but rather fluid and always under construction, the ways in which those constructions get represented are often quite reductive: "The enterprise of constructing ad hoc identities in an immigrant context is a fraught one and the tendency of my ethnographic informants was to repress at least one set of uncertainties by reading the past in coherent, unequivocal, and undoubtedly artificial ways" (31).

According to Ganguly's ethnographic study, it is quite common for Indian immigrants "in a postcolonial context" to feel anxiety about the ways in which the dominant white culture ignores or erases particular distinctions be-tween Indians: "In postcolonial circumstances, the specificity of differences do not matter—the dominant culture does not care whether one is Bengali or Tamil; the relevant criterion of otherness is that Indians are Indians" (37). This, of course, would help to explain Sandeep's apparent discomfort at the science fair that he would be mistaken by the non-Indians for a Googu.

Finally, Ganguly's article also helps to explain the apparent non sequitur in that last paragraph, since much of her scholarship focuses on the tensions and trade-offs that almost all immigrants face in a decision to move to a new culture: is the greater economic opportunity worth the threat to traditional values? In fact, the tension created by this question was at the center of many of the articles I read on Indian-US immigration. For example, in "Guess Who's Coming to Dinner: The Second Generation Is Most Anxiety Ridden Over Dating" (1996), Sunita Sunder Mukhi suggests that many second-generation Indian Americans, while seeking some independence, are determined also to remain Indian and are even willing to acknowledge that their parents play a key role in their decision making: "The control parents exercise over their children is not only economic, but also emotional" since "many Indian Amer-ican youth are burdened by their parents' approval, opinions, and feelings about their circumstances, choices of marriage partners, lifestyles" (2). Accord-ing to Mukhi, the challenge then is to find ways to remain Indian without re-vealing oneself as "too Indian":

> Another aspect of this fear that Indian Americans have is that the part-ner their parents might choose for them would be too desi, too Indian, old-fashioned, tradition bound, tacky. In other words, the potential spouse might speak English with a heavy accent, wear outdated clothes, be stingy with money, and in general ill-equipped to live an urbane In-dian American lifestyle. . . . Being too Indian is like carrying a screaming monkey on your back. Being Indian American is being comfortable, smooth, and cool amidst non-Indianness, in the playing fields of hy-bridity. It is being able to dance the Bhangra unabashedly, wear contem-porary Indian and western clothes smartly, enjoy the pleasures of an urban, cosmopolitan life in New York, as well as in Bombay, London, or Hong Kong, and still care for Mom and Dad (at the very least), and go to the temple on occasion. (4)

Seen in this context (and in the context of contemporary films that deal with Indian immigration, such as *Monsoon Wedding* or *Bend It Like Beckham*), Sandeep's impulse to connect his thoughts about assimilation to comments about money and parental overprotection does not seem out of place or off task at all. The fact that acts of assimilation often lead to economic gain at the expense of cultural loss is a central trope of many or even most immigrant narratives (think, for example, of Richard Rodriguez' *Hunger of Memory*).

My sense, however, is that we rarely do think of our students' essays in the context of published memoirs, critical theory, or extensive research about their subjects. As a result, our readings tend to be flat, uninformed, and unimaginative. I am not suggesting that the only way to read an essay like Sandeep's is to immerse ourselves in long research projects, for I certainly understand that writing teachers do not have the time nor obligation to do this sort of painstaking research for every essay by every student. And I'm also not suggesting that all of the responsibility for redeeming or improving a seemingly boring or disorganized essay rests with the instructor's reading process rather than the student's own writing and revision process. However, the fact that I could not fully understand or perceptively respond to Sandeep's essay until I slowed down, conducted research, consulted with colleagues, and began to look for interesting gaps and tensions in his essay has some serious implications for the way we read all student writing:

- First, this example illustrates what should be a self-evident point: student essays are, in fact, texts. Given the lowly status of the student essay—Robert Scholes argues in *Textual Power* (1985) that student writing has long been dismissed in English departments as "pseudo non-literature"—this assertion has political as well as pedagogical implications. By making the case for student writing as texts worthy of respect, study, interpretation, discussion, and debate, we make the case for our students as writers worth reading and for ourselves as scholars engaged in intellectually rigorous and valuable work. In the current culture of English studies in which everything except the student essay is viewed as a rich text, it is important that we elevate the status of student essays if not to the level of a Keats ode or a Flannery O'Connor story then at least to the level of, say, a Madonna video or a Cosmopolitan ad.

- Second, and this is a related point that should be equally self-evident: reading student essays, which too often is seen as a teacher's most tedious obligation, can be both delightful and instructive. Much of the pleasure of reading a novel or poem or even the daily newspaper comes from discussing—or from the anticipation or memory of discussing—our experience of the text with other readers. While we often get a chance to discuss student essays with our students in a workshop or conference, we very rarely take the opportunity to discuss them with our peers. As a result, we generally miss out on the sort of informed, scholarly, and playful discussion I was able to have with my peers about Sandeep's essay.

- Third, reading Sandeep's essay through the lens of critical theory and research suggests new methods for reading, responding to, and grading student writing. If texts are created as much by readers as by writers—if, as Scholes suggests, what we get out of any reading (whether it is a Toni Morrison novel or a billboard advertisement) is directly proportional to our investment in the interpretive process—it stands to reason that the more time we spend on any student essay, the more interesting it will become. If spending several months reading, researching, and discussing Sandeep's essay led me to understand and appreciate his writing in a new way, we can only assume that this process could—if we suddenly found ourselves with a lot of free time—be replicated with other essays. The most dangerous implication here is that we might actually have to acknowledge that *all* of our students' essays are potentially rich and interesting texts, an acknowledgment with unsettling implications for instruction and grading.

- Finally, this sort of process provides a useful model for ongoing in-service training and faculty development. Just as most social workers and therapists meet regularly to present and discuss difficult cases in order get advice, information, different perspectives, and reality tests, we would benefit from this same sort of collaborative training and support.

So all of this leads me back to my first question: just how many writing teachers *does* it take to read a student essay? I could take a guess, but let me consult with my colleagues and get back to you.

2

Reading and Writing About Death, Disease, and Dysfunction, or How I Spend My Summer Vacations

When I was a first-semester freshman, I went with my roommate to see the dean of students. We had only been in college for eight weeks but we were convinced that we should be allowed to move off campus the next semester. We told the dean that we hated the dorms, the dorm food, the other dorm people. Looking back, I now realize that we were both so afflicted with an overwhelming cynicism, homesickness, and preoccupation with the relationships we left behind that we gave almost no chance to our new acquaintances and surroundings. All we knew was that we would better off in an apartment in town.

I remember the dean looking sad. "I don't understand you kids. When I was a student here, we loved living on the campus. Those conversations we had in the dorm late at the night, I'll tell you, those were the best times of my life. Now I see students, boys and girls, moving into together, I see them using drugs, refusing to get involved in campus life. When I was your age, whenever we were bored, we'd put on a fair or a talent show, or we'd organize a carnival. Whatever happened to good, clean fun?"

We both scoffed on cue.

"So," my friend Gary asked again, "can we move off-campus then?"

Ten years ago, I was hired to design and develop a new writing program for first-year students. I was brought in with a great deal of support and autonomy but also with what I feared were a great number of unrealistically high hopes by faculty across the curriculum: the new program should introduce students to academic discourse and intellectual life; teach them how to use the library, conduct research, and cite sources; and, most of all, make sure that no professor on campus ever had to see another grammatical error or spelling mistake.

31

Haha! Really?

Given the high visibility of this sort of core program, I knew that the one I designed was going to be defined as much by what it wasn't as by what it was. And I knew that it wasn't a lot of things that a lot of people on the campus probably would have liked, including Great Books, essentials of English grammar and usage, critical thinking 101. It was instead a new-fashioned version of an old-fashioned "process" course built around revision, portfolios, workshops, conferences, and the simple notion that student writers should be treated like writers first and like writing students second.

My sense throughout that first year was that things were going reasonably well, at least as much as one person can sense anything that is happening to seventy-five instructors and two thousand students. Still I felt pressure to produce some quick tangible results, something to prove to everyone that the program was working. After all, the university had given me the resources to reduce class size, hire and train good faculty, and provide impressive pastries for our staff meetings.

I can't remember now whether it was I or Eileen Donovan-Kranz, the program's associate director, who played Mickey Rooney to the other's Judy Garland, but I definitely recall that the scene had the feel of an Andy Hardy movie. The only difference was that we changed "I know how we'll get the money to save the school [or farm or family business]: we'll put on a play!" to "I know how we'll raise the cultural capital for our writing program: we'll publish a book of student essays!" I also remember that we both felt a rush of naïve optimism that somehow made us both believe the project would be a snap: we'd invite our first-year writers to submit personal narratives, textual criticism, political arguments, philosophical meditations, and researched essays; organize an editorial board; hire a first-rate art designer; find a publisher; and send out a memo announcing to the staff that the book—we would call it *Fresh Ink*—would be required the next fall in every section of the course.

When summer arrived and we started to read through the year's submissions, I was convinced that our optimism had been justified. The first one was called "Flow" and I was immediately engaged:

> This is not one story,
> but many stories which
> make up what I know of
> my family.

When I was six or seven I lived in a small apartment complex in Acton. I only have a few clear memories from that place. One is a dented, faded red tool box which my brother used as a container for his bottle cap collection. He would occasionally let me look at the caps and I remember how fascinated I was because no two caps were alike. One day I asked him why he had so many beer bottle caps. "Because Dad used to drink," he told me, "You were too young to remember."

That was the first time I
became aware of alcoholism.

(B. D. 1994, 39)

The student author went on to explain how he first became aware of the pattern of drinking and abuse that characterized his father's relationship with his grandfather and, to some extent, his own relationship with his father.

The second essay I read was by a student writing in heartbreaking detail about her eating disorder; the third, a eulogy of a loving grandparent who had recently died. I was excited: this writing was engaging, intense, alive. Assuming that the quality of the other kinds of essays—essays about literary texts, political issues, philosophical ideas—was as good, *Fresh Ink* was going to be a breathtaking success. It would win awards. I would win awards. I would field fan letters from envious writing program directors asking for guidance and advice. I'd go on NPR's *Fresh Air* to talk *Fresh Ink* with Terri Gross.

But as I read through the pile, my anxiety started to grow; there were no essays about literary texts, political issues, philosophical ideas. Or at least not many. Instead, there were dozens, even hundreds, of personal narratives about loss, anger, confusion, and grief. There were suicidal friends and maimed pets, abusive relationships and date rapes, eating disorders and acts of delinquency. There were heartbreaking accounts of growing up in some way different— African American, Latina, Asian American, Jewish, nonathletic, nerdy, fat, four-eyed, a victim of divorce, anything—and feeling forever out of place and out of sorts. There were summer jobs from hell; there were sadistic high school teachers, substitutes, coaches, and administrators (these at least introduced a hint of humor and comic relief); and there was citation-filled page after citation-filled page of research papers on AIDS, HIV, ADD, autism, cancer, Alzheimer's, schizophrenia, obsessive compulsive disorder. What next? Scoliosis? Osteoporosis?

All of these essays about pain and suffering—friends who had moved away, broken down, even done themselves in. Relatives who had died slowly or suddenly, usually not allowing the student enough time to say good-bye. Classmates who had been cruel, vicious, insensitive, bigoted, racist, homophobic, anti-Semitic. Reading all these essays, one after another, felt overwhelming, ominous, even apocalyptic.

What ever happened, I wondered, to good clean fun?

In the summer before I started college, my parents' marriage fell apart. It wasn't the first or the last time—their whole relationship was predicated on melodramatic, near-divorce experiences followed by euphoric, post-near-divorce reconciliations—but that summer my mother's anger reached new heights, her despair sunk to new depths. That summer my parents' marriage imploded in a way that was more extreme than what had come before and less predictable than what would eventually follow.

As the tension escalated, my mother's mood and health grew worse. She began spending more and more time in bed—reading, sleeping, watching TV, and plotting strategy. Sometimes she would call us up to her room and tell us what her lawyer had advised or ask us to speak with my father about his behavior. It was important, she would say, for us to get him to change. While she spoke, I would stare at the pattern of the carpet or the bedspread, trying to disappear, waiting to leave.

Over the years I've grown used to arguments against requiring or even allowing students to write personal essays in a freshman comp course. Critics say that personal narratives are too easy because students have already learned how to write autobiographically in high school or that they are too hard because students so young should not be expected to have a perspective yet on their own life. Or they point out that personal narrative has too little to do with the writing of the workplace or, on the other hand, that it has all too much to do with the bourgeois goal of selling oneself or commodifying one's experience.

How can you still ask students to write personally, a postmodern colleague asked me recently, when we all know that the very notion of a single, unified self is hopelessly naïve and retrograde? When she realized that she was speaking to one of those hopelessly naïve, retro selves, she proceeded to tell me that it was outrageously insensitive "to coerce students into personal revelation in public space"—a rule that applies apparently even if that personal revealer is only a myth, a mask, or a socially constructed representation.

According to the critics of personal writing, our students desperately need all sorts of things: training in literary criticism, the tropes and conventions of academic discourse, cultural studies, postmodern theory, multiculturalism, grammar, usage, critical thinking, library skills. The last thing first-year students need, apparently, is an invitation to tell us or themselves who they were (or who they may still think they are) outside of our classroom.

Even if I granted this point—that we have little to learn from our students or their stories, that they are deficient in so many ways that we can't afford to squander any time encouraging them to talk about their families and friends, their failures and accomplishments, their worst experiences and most nagging doubts—even if I believed all that, I still would wonder how we could expect adolescents, many away from home for the very first time, to move seamlessly from past to present, from parents and siblings and boyfriends and girlfriends and old familiar teachers to unfamiliarity and loneliness and homesickness. Even if I believed that they really did need to know right away about Foucault or syllogisms or socially constructed selves, I'd worry that until they cleared out at least a few of their earlier memories, fears, and fantasies, there just wouldn't be enough room left in their brains.

In the summer before I started college, I received a letter from the Selective Service telling me that I was 1-A. The letter should not have been completely unexpected; after all I was a basically healthy male who unfortunately happened to turn eighteen in that small space of time when the student deferment exemption had ended but the Vietnam War had not. Still this was not supposed to happen. In communities with money and power—and I am still a little ashamed to admit that my hometown had much more than its share of both— getting out of the war was like getting out of jury duty. In fact, I did not at that time know a single person who had gone to Vietnam.

Still I was not sure I wanted to rely on my luck in the lottery, and so I spent part of my summer trying to come up with a fallback plan. I made some inquiries about the possibility of gaining conscientious objector status, but the lawyer I spoke with at the American Friends Service organization advised me that as a nonpracticing, nonbelieving secular Jew, my chances were pretty slim; apparently he was not impressed that I had organized a successful student demonstration in my high school cafeteria, had waited in line three hours to attend the trial of the Chicago Seven, had passed out leaflets for Eugene Mc-Carthy, and knew every word and inflection in every antiwar song by Bob Dylan, Country Joe McDonald, and Phil Ochs. My attempt to get a psychiatric exemption was equally unsuccessful: the psychiatrist I consulted told me, in true Yossarian fashion, that the people *he* was worried about were the ones who *weren't* trying to get out.

Going to war was out of the question, but going to jail or to Canada seemed almost as impossible to a nice suburban kid with a room of his own, an acceptance letter from a liberal arts college, and tickets in hand to see Neil Young and The Who over Christmas break, not to mention a fear of guns, bugs, haircuts, and authority. Still, for some reason—I think it was the fact that I was eighteen—I was irrationally calm about the whole thing. And, sure enough, the week before I left for college, I found help from an unlikely source: I called my allergist to tell him that I needed a letter for the infirmary at college so that I continue to get shots for my hay fever.

"Do you need a letter for your draft board too?"

"Would you write one?"

"Sure," responded my seventy-five-year-old antiwar allergist. "But do me a favor: when you come in for your next appointment, I want you to jog here. No, actually, I want you to run here. And if you have any trouble breathing, don't stop. And don't use your inhaler."

His plan, of course, was to induce an asthma attack, which he would then witness for the sake of the accuracy of the draft board letter. And it worked like a charm. I ran, I had the asthma attack (or something that he led me to believe was an asthma attack), and he wrote such a strong letter unrecommending me for service that even when the members of my dorm gathered in the lobby to listen to the 1971 selective service lottery, even when January 6, 1953, my birthday, came up number 36, I figured I was home free.

For that reason, I was more than a little shocked when I received a letter in my college mailbox notifying me to report in three weeks for an induction physical.

In the second edition of *Fresh Ink,* we published an essay from a student who had witnessed his best friend die in a gang fight, another from a woman who had been beaten up by her boyfriend, another from a student who grew up in Cambodian refugee camps, and still another from a student whose family escaped Vietnam on a makeshift boat:

> After a week of traveling we were still out on the water. Many got seasick. Children cried with hunger. Mothers breast-fed their babies. Siblings held each other the way they never did before. Men tried to be calm and brave. Suddenly, we discovered that there was a small boat within fifty meters of us. We were very afraid. We were stopped by Thai pirates. They were mean and nasty and had weapons on them. Several women immediately hid their gold and jewels in their mouths. My mother had a stomachache but she had to hold back the pain or those pirates might have gotten angry and killed her. All the pirates wanted were gold and jewels. They were very greedy. One girl was raped. One woman got her lips ripped almost in half because she hid her wedding ring and jewels in her mouth. One man got injured badly because he had a gold tooth and a pirate tried to pull it out. We felt lucky that no one was killed. (Anna Hang Ngo 1995, 37)

While very few of the submissions to *Fresh Ink* describe such physical violence, a great many are explorations of emotional trauma. And while an essay about a student's struggle with bulimia or a broken home or a dying grandparent is certainly not the same as being attacked by Thai pirates, it hardly offers much relief.

I don't remember much about my courses my first semester at college, though I do recall that in Freshman English we had to read a book and write a critical essay each week. The first one was about Thucydes' *The Pelopynesian War;* I think we were given a choice of three questions. The second was a comparison of *Antigone* and *The Trial of the Catonsville Nine,* a transcript of the trial of nine people, including Catholic priests Daniel and Philip Berrigan, accused of breaking into a selective service office and burning and destroying files during the Vietnam War. The professor wanted us to think about the relevance of Antigone's appeal that "the laws of god take precedence over the laws of man."

Although my now active selective service file had been transferred from my hometown to the draft board closer to my college, I was never asked to think—by my professor or by myself—whether Antigone's philosophy might shed some light on the decision I was now struggling with or whether my struggle might shed some light on the play. As far as I can recall, my college writing course was my college writing course and my life was my life. And even when my life might have impinged on the text under discussion or the text might have impinged on my life, even, in fact, when we read and discussed Huck Finn, the philosophy remained the same: never the twain shall meet.

I remember feeling surprised and a little horrified that the students who submitted pieces to *Fresh Ink* identified more phases of death and dying than Doctors Kevorkian and Kubler-Ross knew existed in their universe. I wonder now why I didn't expect it. After all, we had asked students in our classes to write what mattered, to take risks, to search for significance, to explore topics about which they still had questions. And what could be more significant and mysterious and risky than death, dying, disease, and dysfunction? So why was I surprised to read so many stories of loss and lack? What did I expect? And what did I crave? I know that I did not crave happy talk about functional families for, as Tolstoy taught us, those families are all boringly alike. It is in the dirt of the details about our common and uncommon suffering that we approach interest and insight.

But did so many of these students have to be so sad, so serious? Did so many have to write about friends who died in car wrecks or committed suicide? About visits to nursing homes to see grandparents and godparents deteriorating with Alzheimer's and cancer? Did so many really have wicked stepmothers, bigoted and insensitive teachers, siblings with autism or AIDS or anorexia?

The irony of all this is not lost on me: here I am asking the same questions of first-year student writers that they are often ridiculed for asking their high school or college teachers after reading *Oedipus Rex* or *Hamlet* or *Beloved.*

Why all this writing about suffering and loss, ambivalence and confusion? Can't we read some happy stories about successful people?

Yeah, why *can't* we? Screw Tolstoy, I could stand to hear about a happy family or two myself.

Since textbook companies and core committees have taken to publishing their plans for how to celebrate diversity and embrace multiculturalism, it was no great surprise to see how many students submitted essays to *Fresh Ink* about their ethnicity and identity. The surprising and distressing part was that so many of these students view their ethnic background as a serious problem, an albatross that has held them back from some sort of social or educational success. A Costa Rican woman complained about friends who innocently told her jokes about Hispanics. A Chinese American woman who has never felt as if she fully belonged in American culture wrote about a trip to China to see her grandparents whom she could barely understand and who referred to her throughout the visit as "the American." A Jewish student described the anger and disorientation he felt on a predominantly Christian campus.

There were a few exceptions. A Puerto Rican woman wrote proudly and nostalgically of her childhood memories of San Juan. A black woman wrote to explain why she resented the mass media's narrow definitions of beauty and why she was proud of her "nappy, natural hair." But, for the most part, students wrote about ethnicity only to describe the pain of feeling foreign in a country in which they were born and the still greater pain of feeling even more foreign when they have visited the country in which their parents were born.

Like many Jews in Russia and eastern Europe early in this century, my grandparents came to America to escape poverty and pogroms; like many Jews growing up in the '30s and '40s in urban America, my parents watched their families go from destitution to a comfortable middle-class life; and like many other Jews of my generation, I grew up rich enough to support my romanticized ideas about poverty (not to mention assimilated enough to support my cynical attitudes about Judaism). By the time I reached adolescence in the '60s, our family tree had been firmly replanted in one of Chicago's leafiest and most desirable suburbs.

Those romantic ideas about poverty kept me from sitting up when I rode in my parents' car (I actually crouched down in the back seat so no one would see my riding in that Cadillac), but they did not keep me from amassing a huge record collection or from choosing to attend a private, expensive college. And these ideas did not seem all that romantic when my father told me that he did not have the money to pay all of my tuition for the second semester. He told me to tell the business office that he needed "to move some money around" and that he would pay them in a few weeks. This came as something of a shock; after all he was a doctor who made a great deal of money. But, as it turned out, he was also an investor in experimental drug companies and South American diamond mines. And during my first semester of college, drugs and diamonds, at least the ones my father chose, were down. Way down.

Not all of the *Fresh Ink* submissions were meant to be depressing or negative. In fact, one of the most common genres was the highly sentimental eulogy for a beloved grandparent. I don't mean to suggest that these pieces were upbeat: in most cases the grandparent in question was quickly deteriorating or, more commonly, recently deceased. But these Nanny or Papa pieces were rarely meant to be tragic or even sad; they were meant instead to be sweet and touch-ing tributes to the one adult who had provided the author unqualified love and a model of how to live.

It has the feel for me of a bad dream: my parents had gone out of town for the weekend and left the four of us—my three brothers and me—in the city with my grandmother. We were not happy about this: my grandmother had always been frantic, controlling, ill-tempered, and, since she spoke in her own hybrid form of part-Yiddish, part-English, part-mutter, part-yell, almost impossible to understand. When my mother was around to translate, deflect, and defend, seeing Nana was fine. But without our buffer, in that small city apartment, it was almost too much for my small suburban sensibility to bear.

Thankfully I've repressed most of it but I do remember her up at the crack of dawn, turning on lights and muttering, "Enough with the sleeping. Up, the Jeffrey Bus, crowded later, a sale Eva told me at Carson's. . . ." And I remem-ber hours of being dragged from store to store, being implored to keep up, being scolded for sitting down on a department store floor. I remember her looking for bargains, crossing items off a list, arguing with sales clerks. And I remember her telling us that if we were good we would get a treat: the treat turned out to be lunch at the Blackstone, an imposing-looking restaurant that had the look of a men's club, with heavy mahogany tables and chairs, waiters in white starched aprons and black bow ties. But we were there because from twelve to two the Blackstone had a special children's meal and price. Though we would have all preferred a hot dog and fries from a streetcorner stand, Nana was set on the good deal at the Blackstone and so there we were, being told, "Boys, presentable, tuck in your shirttails, *again* I have tell you?"

The meal was a disaster. We ordered hamburgers, expecting skinny Mc-Donald's-like patties, but getting instead four-inch-thick ground sirloin. My younger brothers refused to eat it, sending my grandmother into a fit. But just when it looked bleakest, the maître d' came by, sussed out the situation, and came to the rescue. "Here at the Blackstone, we have a policy: if a child finishes his meal, we give him a special prize, a toy. But if he doesn't, no prize." And so Jeff and Dan fought through those monstrous ground sirloins in search of their treasure. When the meal mercifully ended the maître d' returned with the gifts. But just as he reached out to give them to the victors, my grandmother's hand suddenly reached out as well, taking firm possession. "These treats," she told my now tearful little brothers as she held them just out of their reach, "for these, you eat dinner tonight."

Though the sweetness of the grandparent submissions to *Fresh Ink* should have provided some relief in an otherwise bleak landscape, I found the opposite to be true. Of all the submissions, these bothered me most of all. I found myself immediately impatient and dismissive as soon as I read about Poppy's favorite stuffed chair or Grammy's apple turnovers. I found myself doubting that Nanny's eyes always twinkled like a starry night or that Papa always smelled like peppermint.

During her second open-heart surgery, my mother almost died. In fact, three hours into the operation, one of the surgical nurses came out to tell us—my father, aunt, two of my three brothers, my grandmother, and me—that we should prepare for the worst. For a moment, we all just sat there stunned. "Someone should call Dan." My younger brother had been unable to come to Chicago for the surgery and sat thousands of miles ways awaiting some word. Since I was closest to him or maybe just to the telephone, the task fell to me. "Things look really bad, Dan. Mom might not make it thought the surgery," I managed to stammer. Miraculously, though, just an hour later, the nurse was back: "Good news: things went much better that we expected. She's going to make it." This time I jumped for the phone: "Dan, Mom is going to be okay!" In the jubilation of the moment, I noticed the frown on my ninety-year-old Russian Jewish grandmother's face.
   "Who is Lad talking to?" she demanded.
   "He's talking to Dan, Nana," my aunt said gently.
   "*Again* with the long distance calls?" she responded in disgust.

My own stories all have anticlimatic endings: my grandmother, even as she approached one hundred, continued to inspire some of my strongest feelings of frustration and ambivalence. My parents did not divorce. The market for diamonds and drugs picked up.
   And I did not go to Vietnam. Before my induction physical, my parents were able to get my allergist, my pediatrician, and an ears, nose, and throat specialist to write letters testifying to the severity of my asthma (not mention-

ing of course that it was not so severe as to keep me off the wrestling and cross-country teams). When I arrived at the physical, I could not get anyone to tell me whether these letters were in my file or to look at my copies. As the physical and psychological examinations proceeded, I got more and more frantic because, except for the test in which we had to match pictures of tools with their functions, I seemed to passing with ease.

In fact, I seemed to be frighteningly healthy. Unfortunately many of the men there that day were not nearly so unlucky. One guy next to me in line was sent home with a dangerously high fever; his physical was rescheduled for a later date. "Each time before I come here I drink some of my own urine," he whispered to me. "As long as I keep it up, they can't get me." Another unfortunate member of my cohort was sent home when the chest X rays revealed a spot on his lungs. "That's terrible," I stammered. "No, man, it's great. They said they can't take me because it might be malignant. They want me to have it biopsied but if it's benign they'll take me then. Well, I'm not playing their game: I just won't have the biopsy."

At the end of the day, an officer gathered all of us who had passed our physicals. "When you men come back here next month, it will be for induction. Please do not bring any of your own weapons." A few men around me cursed. Others were not about to give up so easily. "What about a pistol?" "What about a bowie knife?" "What about a blackjack?" The officer waved them off. "Men, please, we will supply all weapons." More cursing.

Finally, at the very end of the day, I waited in line to meet with an army doctor. "You have passed all the exams," he told me, "and will be inducted into the US Army next month. Is there any information that you have that would disqualify you for military duty?" With desperate gratitude for the question, I handed him the letters and began to tell him about how useless I'd be in the jungle, about how long it takes me to catch my breath after a jog, about. . . . He waved me off impatiently, read the first paragraph of the first letter, and looked up. "Why haven't you notified the army about your condition before this?"

"I have. I've sent you several letters."

He opened the folder on his desk and thumbed through the papers. Then: "Yes, I see it here. You are 4-F and are not medically fit to serve in the US military. Do you understand?" And he handed me a suitable-for-framing document stating that I could never enlist in the American armed services and told me that I could leave.

By the time the bus dropped me off in town, it was after midnight. I remember thinking that I should feel relieved but all I felt was numb. It was freezing cold, I was four miles from campus, and there were no cabs anywhere in sight. I can't remember how I got back to my dorm but I do remember standing in a phone booth, suddenly feeling overwhelmed with homesickness for a place I no longer considered home.

We often wonder why students hardly ever submit textual criticism for publication in *Fresh Ink*. After all, students in our program often write about poems or stories or films or music or art exhibits. And yet the few submissions that deal with texts seem teacher based, halfhearted, flat.

I don't remember much more about my first semester except that the last three books in my Freshman English course were *Civilization and Its Discontents, No Exit,* and *A Good Man Is Hard to Find*. I remember those three because I somehow convinced the professor that I was being hampered as a writer by the paper-per-week constraint and that, since I had done well on the weekly themes, I should now be allowed to write one longer essay combining all three books. Though I've mercifully managed to repress the details of that composition, I do remember that I put it off until the last moment and then stayed up all night frantically trying to finish. My last foggy memory of that first semester is getting the paper back covered with corrections and a final note from the professor, apologizing: "I'm afraid I let you get yourself in over your head on this one."

I still gasp when I come across a student essay about sexual abuse or date rape, but, on the whole, I have grown harder to shock. I find myself reading more like an ethnographer, noting new patterns and trends. Last year I noted a run of narratives about dying grandparents and lonely first-generation immigrants, while this year's batch seemed heavy on weekend fishing trips with divorced dads and pregnancy scares after drunken unprotected sex.

Still, one trend has not changed: almost all of the student submissions have happy endings. At least that's how they are intended. After detailing a hundred ways that they have been damaged and dissed, scared and scarred, these student authors usually try in the end to put on a happy face. "Now I've learned never to take life for granted." "It's all for the best; you only learn through suffering." "But I know he's in a better place." "I'm glad my father was not like the other fathers; he's special."

Maybe they say such things because they feel guilty about having exposed family secrets. Or maybe because they think we expect essays to have clear resolutions. Or maybe they say these things because this is what they actually believe.

In any case, it is one more problematic feature of the confessional student essay, one more reason that critics often find this form so unsatisfactory. As a group, we academics crave ambiguity, sophistication, doubt, even cynicism.

According to some of my colleagues, recounting a tragic tale and then invoking a pat resolution—"I'm sure it all worked out this way for a reason"—is the stuff of daytime talk shows, not rigorous academic work. I see their point, I suppose. And yet dismissing all of these narratives simply by invoking Oprah or Geraldo seems a lot like a pat resolution too.

The more I remember my own adolescence, the more I watch the world through the eyes of my own teenage daughters, the more I read about mental and physical illness, violence, and tragic loss in Shakespeare and Toni Morrison and the daily newspaper, the less I wonder, first, why so many first-year students choose to write about death, disease, and dysfunction and, second, why they are so eager, even desperate, to repress in the end what they have just written. In fact, I've grown so used to these essays that my question is no longer "Why do they are write about these things?" but "How could they *not* write about them?"

Still this knowledge doesn't make these essays any easier to read. Each summer Eileen Donovan-Kranz, my co-editor, flips frantically through the pile of submissions to *Fresh Ink* muttering, "This year, can we please publish at least one piece about a *functional* family?" Yeah, and after that, maybe we could organize a carnival or put on a fair.

3

Replacing the Carrot with the Couch
Reading Psychotherapeutically

The comedian Jonathan Katz tells a joke that goes something like this: "Don't you hate it when you make a Freudian slip? Just the other day I was out to lunch with my father and I *meant* to say, "Dad, would you please pass the ketchup?" but *instead* I said, "You asshole, thanks for fucking up my entire childhood."

I think about this joke whenever I read the first drafts of my students' personal narratives. What I notice immediately about these essays are the striking differences between what many of my students mean to say—about their families, their feelings, and themselves—and what actually comes out. I've gotten used to these gaps, and I usually find these moments of unself-awareness absurdly and poignantly endearing. There is, for example, the student who, after itemizing in excruciating detail the occasions and events that her father missed over the years—her volleyball games, visitors' days at camp, prom photos, valedictory graduation speech—because he was too drunk to show up, concludes, "Now that Dad is sober, I realize none of that matters anymore."

It is easy to read these gaps and contradictions as logical, even inevitable, marks of compromise, accommodation, and resignation in the face of painful realization. Sometimes, though, the line between compromise and repression, accommodation and denial, is troublingly blurry: for example, there was the essay I received a few years ago from a young woman writing about her success as a cross-country runner. In some ways it is a typical sports narrative. It begins when she is a mediocre runner struggling to make the junior varsity team and ends a year later with her being chosen captain of the varsity. What haunts me is that she attributes her success to the diet she began as a junior when, she says, she was 135 pounds and just too fat to run fast. As her weight dropped—from 135 to 130 to 120 and finally to 105—her time dropped too. Eating only a few crackers, a little plain pasta, a banana, and cup of coffee, she would struggle through the day. But she also says that she loved her new body, loved that there were hollows where there used to be curves, loved that she now felt sleek and strong. And she ends the essay by claiming that her success as a runner as well as her new feelings of self-worth are a direct result of the weight she lost.

I felt the same eerie disconnect between narrative and interpretation when I read an essay by a young man in that same class who was writing about his relationship with his father. That essay begins with the writer explaining how and why his father has been the major influence in his life. He was raised in a poor Irish Catholic family and had worked his way through school to graduate school to a corporate job to finally starting his own very successful business. Along the way, he pushed his son by signing him up for judo and karate and football and summer jobs driving a truck. When he was younger he sometimes didn't understand his father. But when he finally asked why he had to work so hard, his father told him that though the family was well off financially, they were at heart still a blue-collar family. That, he says, is when he realized how hard his father had worked to provide for the family and how much he appreciated his father's insistent lessons.

I am haunted by these essays (even more than others from the same class in which one student wrote about the death of her father and another wrote about a friend who was paralyzed in a car accident) because they seem to contain a large, troubling gap between the student's conscious understanding and unconscious emotion. This kind of contradiction or discontinuity in a student's personal narrative—it usually occurs at the end of the piece—is familiar to writing teachers as a retreat, a summing up, a resolution. "All I know is that I love my father." "My family is different than other families but we're different in a good way." "Now I know that Jack died for a reason." The gap is the denial of something I know the writer knows but won't let herself say or even feel. I am, of course, unsettled when one of my students describes an eating disorder or admits to resenting a parent. But I am far more unsettled when they deny what they have just confessed.

These gaps—between the student's conscious understanding and unconscious emotion and between what it is explicitly stated in the text and what I think it represents—are always tricky to talk about directly. In fact, I usually respond to these gaps in writing conferences in a fairly nondirective way, hoping to lead the student to see meaning behind contradictions. Usually they don't. Conferences with these student writers are, I imagine, like conferences would be with Huck Finn or Emma Woodhouse or maybe the butler in *The Remains of the Day*: I am constantly aware of how the text reveals more to me about them than they realize about themselves—and constantly aware that it would awkward and painful for me to tell them so.

There is often humor in the self-deceptions of fictional characters, but with these students I usually feel more like I am stuck teaching Bartleby, Melville's depressed and depressing enigmatic character, who would only say "I prefer not to" when asked to write, act, respond, or explain. What I mean is that the students often exhibit an amazing and provocative passive resistance and seem oddly disassociated from the story they are telling. In the presence of these unreliable narrators, I struggle to retain my professional distance, trying to wake them up, trying not to panic or judge, but feeling increasingly irritated, baffled, and ultimately somehow guilty. Melville's narrator, who finally can't stand the tension and has Bartleby removed from his job, evicted from his office, arrested for loitering, and eventually committed to a mental hospital, is certainly not the role model I want to follow in these instances. But who is my role model and what is my role when I am faced with these students?

These are the sorts of questions that fuel the debate in universities about the boundaries between writing instruction and psychotherapy. Because these students and these questions make us so anxious, some writing teachers will say only, "Focus on the writing. That is what we are trained and paid to do, not to behave as frustrated therapists." But what does that mean in these cases? It is not a matter of simply deciding to focus on rhetoric or psychology, on the writing or the writer. The lines are always blurred. One inevitably leads to the other. The gap in the essay is to some extent the gap that always exists between a writer and reader, an utterance and an interpretation.

The truth is that the jobs of the writing instructor and psychotherapist are never so clearly defined as that neat binary suggests: both disciplines are concerned with helping others make unconscious material conscious. Just as it is dangerous and naïve to assume that we can cure this student's eating disorder, it is also dangerous and naïve to assume that we can ignore it. The essay, the situation, the student, demand a response and, given the nature of the essay, at least part of that response will exist in the margins between writing instruction and psychotherapy. That makes most writing teachers anxious. I still remember a writing program administrator I once worked for who told his staff, "When one of your students writes a troubling essay, do three things: refer, refer, refer." But referring (and, by implication, pathologizing) can be as fraught, perhaps more fraught, than not referring.

Focusing only on the grammar or mechanics or structure of the sort of essays I described a moment ago is as inappropriate as throwing aside the essay and saying, "Now let's get to work on that eating disorder." What we can do is not unlike what a therapist does—focus on the material itself, on the narrative that the student or patient brings to us, focus on details. In this way, we can approach the messy and elusive psychological issues through specific questions about our experience as readers of the text, and we can respond in open-ended ways that invite further introspection: "I hear the essay saying. . . ." "Readers might think that. . . ." "This part does not match with this part. Why not?"

With the runner's essay, my impulse was to help her see how her text might affect readers—and in fact my sense turned out to be right, for when she read it to her peers in a writing workshop, most were greatly disturbed by it. Many were angry with the writer. "When I read the first few pages of your essay, I loved it," one of them said. "I even was thinking that I wanted to send it to my friend who had an eating disorder because I thought it would help her. I thought at the end you were going to say that you know now that you have a problem and you are getting help. But you don't even admit you have a problem. I wouldn't even show it to my friend now. It gives the wrong message." My hope was that she would realize that the central power was in her ability to show how and why her starvation felt empowering, even transcendent, but that power would be compromised if she didn't also show or at least suggest that she knew what she was doing to herself and that she knew readers probably didn't understand.

Here psychotherapeutic models can't help but inform our thinking. When students write radically personal or confessional essays, they are bound to stir up powerful responses in their readers and in themselves. And though everyone—students, writing teachers. administrators—gets squeamish about the mere mention that this process is psychotherapeutic, there's no way around the fact that psychotherapy is the field that best prepares us to think about these issues; in the case of the two essays I described, for example, most of my assumptions come from psychotherapeutic models, such as:

- The gap between what a text says, the manifest content, and what a text means, the latent content, is usually created by the gap between the writer's conscious knowledge and unconscious motives and associations.

- In spite of what managed-care companies believe, this unconscious material cannot always be easily and quickly accessed. In fact, students are often not ready to confront this material, which is why the gap exists in the first place.

- A writer's failure to respond to suggestions about closing the gap in an essay could have more to do with psychological resistance than rhetorical limitation.

- On the other hand, a teacher's sense that there is a gap that needs to be addressed could have nothing to do with a student's resistance and everything to do with the teacher's own unresolved issues that have somehow been stirred up by the essay or by the student; in other words, a perceived gap in a student's essay could be the result of our own unresolved countertransference issues.

- Though a student may feel some relief and catharsis simply because she has related a traumatic experience, she may also feel some shame or secondary trauma about the public nature of this confession. Given that possibility, it is important not to push students too hard to confront or analyze material that makes them uncomfortable.

For these reasons, I assumed that if the runner could acknowledge her psychological issues, if she could recognize and name them ("I cringe when people say I have an eating disorder," she told me in a conference), understand them more fully, the gap would begin to close and her own control as a writer would increase. And, though I know how grandiose this sounds, I also hoped that closing this gap might help her gain some control of her eating disorder, just as I hoped that the boy's essay and his psyche would be helped if I gave him permission somehow to be angry at his father.

I realize that this kind of thinking can be risky for a teacher who does not have the professional training, mandate of the university, or consent of the student to turn a writing course into psychotherapy. But since we do have the training, mandate, and consent to advance and complicate our students' usual ways of thinking, reading, and writing, our roles and boundaries will occasionally get blurred. There is no moment when I would ever say to a student, "I notice that there is always a mother figure hovering in the background of your essays; why do you think that is?" or "To improve this essay, you need to confront the transference emotions that are obviously being stirred up in our relationship." But, as a writing teacher who firmly believes that we ought to allow students to write autobiographically and that we ought to pay more attention to the role of the unconscious in the composing process, there are plenty of moments when I sense that I am being pulled into the role of parent, confidante, therapist.

Stepping over these boundaries can be risky, but so, too, is the urge to run away from the personal, to pretend that nothing is happening at these charged moments. To offer no response to a provocative, emotional, confessional essay is to offer a very powerful response, as is the immediate decision to refer the student to someone else for counseling. To make psychotherapy the focus of our instruction is, of course, dangerous and inappropriate; but to design a first-year writing course that strives to eliminate opportunities for psychological confession and introspection by deemphasizing all forms of personal writing seems a damaging overreaction.

Many critics of writing courses in which students write autobiographical essays and thus cross boundaries between school and life, personal and public, writing and therapy, forget that we got to this point because so many of us had grown disenchanted with the detached, disembodied writing and reading of the preprocess composition classroom. Early experts in the field such as Don Murray, Peter Elbow, Janet Emig, and Ken Macrorie identified what was wrong with a dreary, dismal writing curriculum and fixed it with the most daring, innovative, and elegantly simple solutions: let the students choose what to write about; open up space and give them encouragement to write about what matters to them; emphasize the role of discovery and the unconscious in invention and drafting; read and listen for significant details but also for what is not yet there on the page; respond in nondirective, open-ended ways; focus more on the writer than the writing; give the writer real readers, including peers; give the student the incentive and opportunity and skills—help them develop a process—they can use after the class is over.

Teaching in this way does increase the likelihood that students will write daring and provocative pieces. And it's probably true that a writing teacher who is interested in his own inner life is more likely to get essays from his students about theirs. Still I don't coerce my students into confessional writing, though critics of personal writing think those of us who get essays about death, dying, and dysfunction must stand up in front of the class and announce, "For a C, I need to see alcoholism or abuse; for a B, the death of a parent; and, for an A, there'd better be blood on the page." In the words of Alicia Silverstone's character in the movie *Clueless:* "As if!" The reality is that there are always some students in a class who are so eager to tell someone about where they've been, what they've been through, they will do so by leaping into the smallest space at the slightest invitation.

It seems to me that writing teachers who deny any connection between writing instruction and psychotherapy protest too much: no one claims that writing instruction equals therapy; even if we're talking about writing instruction that emphasizes personal narrative, free-associative invention exercises, and self-actualization and that employs process-oriented, conference-based, nondirective methods, we know as writing teachers that we are not therapists. And if we ever forget, our fee structures are sure to remind us. But the fact that the two fields are not identical in their goals is not the point. I'm not looking here for an exact match, just for productive intersections. It simply makes sense when we confront difficult issues in writing instruction to turn to a field based on helping people get access to their unconscious; on negotiating dyad relationships; on the nature and value of self-analysis; on overcoming resistance to discovery and change; on the significance of details in language and action; and on the relationship between interpretation, response, and revision.

We need to learn to rely much more heavily and strategically in our teaching on our own unconscious. Janet Emig's "The Uses of the Unconscious in the Composing Process" was a landmark essay, because it pushed us be-yond an emphasis on conscious, deliberative, visible steps or techniques of composition—such as outlining or proofreading—to the unconscious, less visible or obvious processes—such as what is happening when a writer finds a topic, comes to an insight, connects one idea to another, gets blocked or un-blocked. What followed—the teaching and use of freewriting, the assigning of journals, letters, and personal narratives, the attention to the benefits of the one-to-one conference—were acknowledgments of the significance of the writer's unconscious, particularly in the early stages of composing. What didn't follow, oddly enough, were acknowledgments of the significance of the *teacher's* unconscious.

This strikes me as odd, first, because it would seem to follow logically that if the production of text is at least partially an act of the unconscious then the consumption or interpretation of that text is, too. Robert Bly's description of the relationship between a poet and his reader as "inside talking to inside" could—or should—apply to the relationship of the first-draft writer and her composition instructor.

However, if we ever acknowledge the role of our own unconscious in reading, interpreting, and, most of all, evaluating student writing, it is to offer apologies or a blanket warning: be careful not to impose your own issues onto a student's writing. Our goal then is to strive for a kind of neutrality that seeks to deny or control any countertransference emotions stirred up by the student or the text. The question we ask ourselves is not *how can I use my unconscious as a valuable tool to make sense of this text?* but rather *how can I monitor or po-lice myself so that my unconscious will not get in the way of my objectivity and self-control?* In this rigid model, the only tool that will allow us to make sense of, respond intelligently to, and fairly evaluate the student essay is our con-scious mind, when in fact it stands to reason (especially to those of us inter-ested in psychoanalysis) that the unconscious plays a central and critical role in reading, interpretation, learning, insight, response, and evaluation.

To take fuller advantage of our unconscious, we need to borrow lessons from psychoanalysis. The analyst, as Freud explains in *Recommendations to Physicians Practicing Psychoanalysis* (1912), must listen in an open-ended way with his or her "analyzing instrument," that is, must "turn his own uncon-scious like a receptive organ to the transmitting unconscious of the patient. He must adjust himself to the patient as a telephone receiver is adjusting to the transmitting microphone" (115). I recognize that this is a counterintuitive method for most writing teachers: we try so hard—too hard—to be smart, at-tentive, helpful, and on task that we fail to read and listen between the lines. For to be truly open to this sort of communication, we need to give up some degree of control. "Central to this mental set," the psychoanalyst Ted Jacobs

(1991) explains, "is a valuable degree of regression in both participants. This state of regression, which is a necessary condition in patient and analyst alike for understanding the unconscious connections of the other, is closely allied to the kind of ego-regression that occurs in the artist during moments of creative activity" (119).

Of course, the process of reading and responding must involve some significant attention to the actual words of the student's text, but it must involve, too, some attention to the student's latent meaning, some attention to our own internal associations and responses, and somehow a suspension of critical activity around these observations. Again, to accomplish this requires some letting go and giving up of ego and control. The analyst Karen Horney (1999) describes a way of listening to a patient that we can adapt to the student and her text:

> Wholeheartedness of attention means being there altogether in the service of the patient, yet with a kind of self-forgetfulness. This may sound contradictory: being there with all your faculties and yet forgetting yourself. Still if you think of the many situations in which somebody operates with ultimate effectiveness, you will see there is no contradiction. The goal is to self-forget but be there with all of your feelings. You know that one can be emotionally absorbed by a picture or piece of music, or something on stage by nature, and at the same time almost forget oneself. This kind of observing makes no sense unless we add one factor: Don't select too early. . . . If you need to know and understand everything too quickly you may not see anything. I am not just speaking of the need to interpret to the patient. If you must have something in your mind because of your own insecurity or intellectual pride, then you may just need to have quick labeling, which means that the comprehensiveness of your listening is bound to suffer. (188)

Though we claim to resist these sorts of lessons from psychotherapy because we want to protect our students, I suspect that we are actually more worried that this approach would force us to analyze our own gaps and forms of resistance. In fact, I am not suggesting that a writing teacher should play therapist; I am suggesting that we should play patient.

For example, back to that essay about the pushy, aggressive father: why did this narrative affect me so strongly? I pitied the blue-collar son for his situation but I was also angry at him for his lack of understanding and, even more, for his lack of anger. Why was he so passive? Why did he feel he needed to apologize for and defend his father? Why did he say that he owed his father so much? I'll tell you what I felt he owed him: he owed him a kick in the ass. Let his father go out for football or sign up for goddamn taekwondo. Let him deal with a father who offered his teenage son judgment in the place of un-qualified love. It was only at this point in my rant that it began to occur to me that this all sounded sickly familiar, that I had felt this way many times before in my own life. But this couldn't be about me, could it? My own father wasn't the first-generation son of Irish Catholic immigrants; no, he was the first-generation son of Russian Jewish immigrants. And he didn't work his way out of poverty into corporate life. He came out of poverty to become a doctor. And he didn't make me do judo and football, but he *was* passionately and ir-rationally involved in my career as a high school wrestler. Suddenly I couldn't be so smug about those psychic gaps in my students' papers.

When I reread my student's essay, I did not find his portrait of his father nearly as negative as I had remembered it. Now I am not saying that all of the anger I identified in his essay came only from my own projections, but let's just say that when I go out to lunch with my father there have been times when I meant to say, "When I was a teenager, you could have been more supportive and affectionate," but all these years later it still comes out, "Please pass the ketchup." What I am suggesting is that personal writing stirs up teachers as well as students, and if we are going to respond responsibly we need to inves-tigate our own unconscious biases and associations.

While I'm on the topic and in the spirit of honest disclosure, risk-taking, and self-awareness, let me go back to something I just said: my father is not just any old doctor; he's a (and here there should be a drum role or at least a change in the lighting) psychoanalyst. I realize the riskiness of revealing my father's job at this point in a chapter about the value of psychotherapeutic models for writing teachers: I realize that you might now be thinking (to quote a line from the cult classic *Ferris Bueller's Day Off*): "Oh, so *that's* the way it is in their family." I hope that what I'm arguing for here is not just about the needs of one neurotic teacher who is really a frustrated therapist or, even worse, an ex-tended Oedipal struggle to prove that, though I get paid much less for my fifty-minute hour than my father gets paid for his, my work is just as valuable. In other words, my confession that I am the adult child of a psychoanalyst might create a credibility problem for me here.

But I feel a need to acknowledge to you and to myself that my own ap-proach, my advocacy for a psychotherapeutically oriented approach to writ-ing instruction, grows out of a very particular background and context and that this is a particular language and way of thinking that is not for everyone. (I'm reminded suddenly of another Katz joke. He says that he quit therapy be-cause he didn't think his therapist had the stomach for the job: "Whenever I started to talk about something painful, he'd hold up his hands; 'Let's not open up *that* can of worms.'"). I am not interested in being evangelical. Some peo-ple don't want to cross this border, and in fact, if they believe that they are not psychologically equipped to cross it, then they probably shouldn't. But I'm convinced that some of us can and should responsibly make use of psychotherapeutic models in the process of reading and responding to student writing.

I'm convinced of that even though, for some time, I have faced critics in print and in the hallways of my own department who believe that students should not write confessional essays and writing teachers should not play therapist. My most defensive response is to attribute my critics' disdain for the personal to their own unresolved issues about their own childhood experiences. But when I am honest, I admit that my commitment to this kind of personal writing and teaching *does* have a great deal to do with my own family background. I grew up in a family that embraced self-analysis and the unchallenged assumptions that slips and dreams and forgetting were the result of our own unconscious motivations. About the only thing we did not analyze fully was our commitment to analyzing everything fully.

I realize that the danger of this style, like the danger of any other style, is that those who adopt it can become blind to alternatives and can come to see our own way of proceeding as normal and natural. People I met when I was a teenager used to say, "Your father is a psychoanalyst? How awful! Didn't he try to analyze you all the time?" I'd respond "How naïve! You can't analyze your own family. Even Freud admitted that. My father never analyzed my brothers or me. When we talked he would just sit and listen and show no emotion except to occasionally frown or occasionally murmur a cryptic mm-mm or occasionally ask why we forgot to do something he desired or ask our motivation when we did something he disapproved of. Did he psychoanalyze us? Please! My brothers and I were the ones who did all the talking. We were the ones who kept trying to figure out what he was thinking, what we needed to do to please him. We were the ones who analyzed ourselves; he hardly said anything. It was *nothing* like therapy." How's *that* for a psychological gap?

I want to believe that my childhood training—being brought up to accept *The Interpretation of Dreams* like a Southern Baptist accepts the Bible—just gave me the skills that any good writing teacher (and any good literary scholar) needs—the ability to think heurmenuetically and psychodynamically, to read between the lines, to listen to what is not being said, to look for patterns and connections and hidden likenesses, to pay attention to the smallest details. But that would be disingenuous: I know that my overdetermined commitment to a particular way of reading and responding to student writing grows in large part out of my own quirky background.

The other reason I brought up my father's profession is that I think it is important to take risks. Therapists and writing teachers both argue that people should take risks but we rarely model or perform risk taking ourselves. So while I am on the topic, let me confess that what I do as a writing teacher also has a great deal to do with my experience as a psychotherapeutic patient. And I have a *lot* of experience. In fact, not only have I been in therapy for the past ten years, for the last three years I have been seeing two therapists, using the second one to help me work through what I've figured out from the first. I know this seems a bit absurd but once you get into therapy as deeply as I have it's not easy to get out. In fact, I have planned to quit for a number of years, but in the words of Michael Coreleone (as played by Al Pacino in *Godfather III*), "Every time I try to get out they keep pulling me back in." And *he* was only trying to get out of the Mafia.

My point is that watching myself as a patient—along with reading psychoanalytic theory and growing up as the son of an analyst—has contributed to the way I read and respond to student writing. Let me mention just a few of the specific strategies I've been able to adapt to my teaching. First, my own experience in therapy has taught me that always trying to be a good patient, always trying to meet or surpass what you take to be someone else's expectations, can backfire. At certain points in the process, such as moments of insight and discovery, trying to be reasonable or fair or likeable can get in the way when it would be better to quit thinking so much about audience, logic, propriety. In other words, being smart and controlled is not always the best path to insight and learning. Second, my therapy has taught me that strategically timed interruptions can be very useful. Therapists interrupt patients when they fall into repetition that allows them to avoid getting to central issues. At first those interruptions made me mad (I would think and occasionally even say, "Why don't you try acting like a psychiatrist and just listen?"), but then I grudgingly understood. Now I appreciate and even count on being forced to stop and examine a pattern I keep falling into.

I've learned, too, to free-associate more as a reader and listener. In a response to a draft, I am now more apt to say something like, "As I read your essay, I had this image in my mind . . ." or, "This may be way off but I just connected what you're saying to. . . ." I am more apt to rely on symbolism and, following the lead of some psychoanalysts, I am more likely to rely on metaphorical rather than directive language. Again, I am not suggesting here that we should use these strategies to "do therapy" in our classrooms or to insist that our students confront and reveal material they have repressed. In fact, I've learned that even the best suggestions and questions might be ignored, that people can only go as far as their own defenses will allow, and that we need to be patient enough to understand that a writer, like a patient, might not be ready to write the narrative that we think or hope is lurking just beneath the surface.

I am suggesting, though, that it can valuable to help students gain access to and control over unconscious material and that we shouldn't be afraid or reluctant to provide support and opportunity to students ready and eager to engage in that process. Several years ago I wrote in a book that I disagreed with the literary critic Louise Rosenblatt when she said that English teachers should not play therapist and "should not meddle with their students' emotional lives." I wrote that I *want* to meddle with my students' lives and I want them to meddle with *mine.* Though I regret using language that made me sound like Wicked Uncle Ernie from *The Who's Tommy,* I would still make the same case for the importance of depth in student writing and emotional intensity in the teacher-student relationship. Though it can be scary and risky to teach in this way, I *want* to open that can of worms. And I want to quit apologizing, feeling defensive, or being evasive about it. Yes, it fulfills some of my own needs and, yes, it grows to some extent out of my own idiosyncratic background and temperament. But there are by now generations of people who have taught or taken such a course who can offer passionate testimony in defense of the personal and psychological—as well as the academic—benefits of this approach.

I am tired of apologizing for teaching writing in a way that I hope fundamentally changes my students and myself. I am tired of being defensive because some of my students have had sad or hard or painful experiences and choose to tell me and their classmates about those experiences. I am tired of apologizing that I allow, even encourage, my students to write occasionally in first person; after all, first person worked pretty well for Montaigne and Thoreau, Forster and Freud, Baldwin and Woolf. Most of all, I am tired of being defensive about something we ought to be proud of—the way our field, like psychotherapy, can help people make sense and gain control of their personal as well as their public lives.

4

Car Wrecks, Baseball Caps, and Man-to-Man Defense

The Personal Narratives of Adolescent Males

As soon as Tim Flanagan skipped the second class of the semester, I had him pegged as a problem to be endured rather than a student to be taught. "Hey, Professor [the day he missed I had asked them to call me by my first name], you're probably wondering where I was Thursday? *Third* row tickets to U2 Wednesday night. You couldn't expect me to give that up, could you?" I should have asked right then what Wednesday night had to do with Thursday morning or joked about lowering his grade for not getting me a ticket to the concert or said that, yes, I did expect him to give it up if he couldn't make it to class otherwise. But, for some reason, I just shrugged, smiled sickly, and muttered, "No, I guess not." I did decide on a strategy for dealing with Tim, though: I would just ignore him, plow ahead, and make him the first volunteer in my personal struggle to stem grade inflation.

"I asked you to bring in your first drafts of your personal narratives. Would anyone be willing to read your essay aloud so we can discuss it in a workshop?" To my surprise, Tim was the only one who raised his hand. I hadn't thought he had even written an essay. "I'll read mine but [here he paused to smile] is it okay if my essay is about something illegal?" I responded with that same inarticulate shrug, mumbled, "I guess," and waited for another of those male narratives that I have come to hate—another why-I-should-be-admired-for-getting-drunk-and-getting-into-a-near-fatal-car-crash or what-was-so-funny-about-that-time-me-and-my-friends-played-a-great-Halloween-prank-on-the-class-nerd. Sure enough, my first impression of the opening paragraph of Tim's narrative about his success as a shoplifter was that it seemed self-congratulatory, vaguely antisocial, and stylistically Hemingwayesque; that is, it seemed embarrassingly male:

It was a game we played. I'd show up about a half hour after school. Never sooner, never later. Those were the rules. He'd be there, usually hanging around the register, stuffing bags or authorizing checks or just waiting, I'd stroll in through the automatic doorways. I'd pause to read the announcements on the bulletin board. That's rule #18 of shoplifting. I did it so he could see me and prepare for the game. I knew he was watching. I knew he was probably wishing that I was older so he could punch the shit out of me. But he had to stay within the rules. His own rules. The rules he established and the rules he lived by. We rarely made eye contact but we are always aware of each other's presence. He the stern store manager and me the young hoodlum.

As I reread this now, I can see that in many ways—in fact, in most ways—Tim's essay is not typical or conventional. It does not seem pat or predictable (there is a provocative and potentially powerful tension between the dangerousness of the situation and the jocularity of rule #18, for example), and it has a kind of consciousness and control in the narrative that most young male writers aim for but usually miss. Significantly, though, my first reaction was to read Tim's essay and the epic struggle he was setting up with the store manager through the lens of so many other male hero-as-antihero narratives that I have learned or grown to resist.

But it wasn't just my problem with the genre that got in the way. I was not ready or able to see much of the honesty, skill, or promise in that paragraph because I was not ready to see much of the honesty, skill, or promise in Tim. And that goes back not only to what he did—skipping one class, coming into the next one five minutes late, and then, without worrying that he had missed anything significant, theatrically volunteering to read his illegal narrative—but also to problems that I have had with certain male students throughout the years. Like many teachers, I find I often have trouble with male students because they are either too aggressive or too passive; but unlike many teachers who feel this way for personal and perhaps unfair reasons, I resented Tim Flanagan for perfectly legitimate ones:

- He almost always wore a baseball cap.
- I heard from a colleague that he was obnoxious.
- He was a sophomore who—because he had transferred into our university after his first year—was now disrupting the usual classroom dynamics of my freshman class.
- I knew he was in a fraternity, because one day I saw him, wearing a blue blazer, red tie, and satisfied expression, make another student, wearing a clown outfit, do fifty pushups.

And so as I listened to Tim read his narrative, I listened for error rather than for potential. And when he got to the second paragraph I started to find some evidence to support the negative conclusion that I had actually already reached:

> His name was Leo. I know because his picture hung above the service counter entrance. "Store Manager" was his title although I just thought of him as the enemy, the establishment, the order. He was Italian in name and looks. He had that dark complexion and black hair. I remember his face: stern and unfriendly, almost angry. He always wore the same ugly clothes. A brown tie and oxford and brown pin striped pants. He had a slight belly and slouched shoulders. He always carried a small notebook and pen in his ear.

I was put off by what I took to be the snotty, self-satisfied, middle-class portrait of Leo's working-class, Italian status and by the way Tim's portrait of "the enemy" reminded me of other narratives written by other problematic male students—narratives about overcoming impossible odds and performing with grace under fire, narratives that start, for example, like this one:

> The game had more meaning than the average championship match because we had lost to the same team one year earlier. Once again we were billed as the underdogs, and it seemed as though we were out to prove something more because the other team was stacked with so many good players. Their forwards were the fastest in the whole league and they had two huge defensemen who would smash you against the boards any chance they got.

In other words, they are narratives that focus in clichéd language on acts of machismo. And though there are many male students who do not write in this form and some female students who do, there seems to be a general understanding in the field, supported by most of the published literature, that these narratives constitute a common genre of adolescent male writing: Geoffrey Sirc (1989), in his analysis of "male topic features," observes that these essays often deal with the author's mastery of an "epic" experience—often a "quest or mission"—in the "apocalyptic" tone of "pulp" fiction (5); Linda Peterson (1991), borrowing one of her student's descriptions, refers to young men's stories of "wild canoe trips" that have "the fine echoes of Miller's beer commercials" (175); Elizabeth Flynn (1988) maintains that many male narratives, such as a description of a solo airplane flight or of a high school swimming career, "are stories of individual achievement or frustrated achievement and conclude by emphasizing separation rather than integration or reintegration into the community" (429); and almost every-one writing on this topic notices that these narratives almost never include female figures but quite often include strong male figures that the isolated male narrator must react against.

The usual professional response to these conventional narratives—after pointing out that essays that uphold gender stereotypes are problematic whether they deal with male or female roles, whether they are written by men or women—is to suggest the need for more class discussion of gender difference and behavior (Flynn 1988, 432); for designing and evaluating assignments in ways that do not privilege one sex over the other (Peterson 1991, 175); and, perhaps, for encouraging students to experiment more in their writing with cross-dressing (Peterson 1991, 178) and code switching (Sirc 1989, 10).

Though I, too, have noticed these patterns and endorsed similar suggestions, I still worry about positing notions of gender that seem fixed and monolithic, notions that by ignoring class, culture, race, ethnicity, sexual preference, and individual difference seem to move inevitably toward essentialism. Once we begin with the assumption, for example, that men do not value intimacy or connection or that women have trouble acting independently or assertively, our readings of student texts can easily become reductive and self-fulfilling prophecies. In an insightful extension of the previous literature on this topic, Don J. Kraemer (1992) suggests that our usual coding or identification of essays according to gender categories is often misleading or simplistic. In his readings of two essays, one by a male and one by a female, he shows how conventional readings overlook the complexity and subtle code switching that occurs. In other words, an essay about the schoolboy football victory may focus on an act of achievement and success but may also contain significant indications of doubt and insecurity.

Still, a male writer's choosing to write about doubt or insecurity or about the desire for intimacy by writing about football or shoplifting is significant—and, I think, problematic. For my sense is that many composition teachers—*male as well as female*—have largely negative reactions and particular resistance to the conventional male narrative. I know this resistance through my own personal experience as a writing teacher—I've always found the men who write about car wrecks, sports, and male bonding to be among the most difficult I teach, and I've always found their rough drafts among my least favorites in the class—but I also know it through the stories, reports, and questions of the teachers who work in the writing program that I direct. At our annual "papers from hell" staff meeting—I invite faculty to bring in the kind of essays that they least like to read—there is always a wide range of dreaded genres represented, including the author-vacated research paper, the politically incorrect persuasive essay, and the plot summary response to a literary text, but each year the conventional male narrative is right up—or down—there with the worst of them. (Such negative reactions may go far to explain the documented gender discrepancy in grades: in "Gender and Teacher Response to Student Writing" (1992), Duane Roen cites eight separate studies demonstrating that "our grading, especially at the secondary level, has tended to favor females over males" (127–28).

Some of these males' essays are conventional success stories—like scoring the winning touchdown or run in a big high school game—that seem to the instructor to have no insight or point beyond the narrator's desire to say, "Look at this great thing I did before I came here to college." That seems, surprisingly enough from a middle-class adult perspective, anyway, to be the same motivation for the conventional delinquency papers—the time the narrator and his buddies "got ripped and trashed a golf course just for the hell of it" or the time the narrator and his friends decided to get back at a cranky middle-aged neighbor who complained that their music was too loud by tipping over his car. These stories are told with pride and (though I read them in a grim and tight-lipped way) a sense of humor. Reductively, I plugged Tim's essay into this genre, though as I look back now at his draft I see how difficult it is to reduce:

> I always walked around the store one time before the game actually started. It wasn't very big but it was big enough. Sometimes when he lost me I would sneak into the produce section and look through the one-way mirrors at him. It was the only safe haven in the store where I could see him and he couldn't see me. I could look in his eyes. He tried to look unobvious and relaxed, talking to customers, but he was always sweating and constantly scanning the aisles. I used to think about him a lot then. Was he married? Did he have kids? Was he happy? I could have almost felt sorry for him but emotions weren't part of the game. They could make you lose your touch and that could be dangerous.

[margin annotation: has feeling *]*

Tim's provocative questions about Leo should have led to provocative questions of my own. Was this a narrative about shoplifting? About mastery? About individuation? Or was it about Tim's relationship to Leo? About what connects and isolates men from one another? Instead, because I was irritated by his tone and the fact that he made Leo sweat, I listened with my arms tightly crossed and my jaw clenched. I have run into this problem before: several years ago, I published an article in *College English* about the problems that I had with several passively aggressive eighteen-year-old males whom I identified by their baseball caps, high-topped sneakers, smirkiness—and by their self-congratulatory writing. I suggested that I felt inappropriately angry at these males and that my anger kept me from reading their essays with generosity, creativity, or enthusiasm. Though that part of my essay was admittedly quirky and confessional—and though I attributed much of the problem to my own neuroses and insecurities—I received a number of letters, phone calls, and email responses from male and female teachers suggesting that I was not alone in my experience or response: apparently, these passively aggressive herd-instinct young men who write about sports successes, acts of delinquency, and conquests of nature populate composition courses across the country and, apparently, they create anger, frustration, and resistance in a significant number of college writing teachers.

So why *are* these essays so difficult for so many of us to read and like? And why do so many of us resist the details, ethos, and worldview they present and represent? When I asked that question of faculty members who teach in our first-year writing seminar, they offered three common explanations: first, they suggested, these essays just are not very good—predictable, superficial, and unsophisticated. Second, since male authors are often more difficult to work with—less open to negotiation, more resistant to revision—a writing teacher anticipates trouble and thus reads these drafts with conscious and unconscious anxiety and anger. And finally, since these essays often focus on acts of machismo; often glorify aggression, competition, and male bonding; and usually fail even to acknowledge the existence of women, the teacher-reader encounters a text that seems to reflect, support, and promote an androcentric and, to some extent, misogynist agenda.

While all of these explanations sound reasonable, they reveal as much about our limitations as about the limitations of our male students. To say that these male narratives are predictable, superficial, or unsophisticated only begs the question. Most first drafts by first-year students, whether written by males or females, whether dealing with an experience as a volunteer in a homeless shelter or a star of a high school football game, initially seem, well, like first drafts by first-year students: predictable, superficial, unsophisticated. In most cases, however, we use our skill, experience, and imagination to read (or misread) these drafts in productive ways; that is, we have learned to listen to what is not yet being said and to read through the text for meaning, nuance, tension, potential.

However, because we are bothered by the implicit and explicit politics of characteristically male essays, by the ethos that is being created and exalted, we become resisting readers, unable or unwilling to read behind and beneath the conventions that these men choose or are chosen by. We are often too quick to imagine in male narratives a lack of ambiguity, complexity, or doubt. Or put another way: we too often read male narratives as fixed, reifying our own interpretations, acting as if the meaning of a text can somehow be read right off the page. Our readings ironically reproduce the problem: in the face of these male narratives and their authors, we, too, become passive aggressive; that is, we too hold back and become predictable, superficial, unsophisticated.

Though most of us are usually expert at "reading for discontinuity" (Kraemer 1992, 331) in student texts, we often fail to do so when confronted by heavily gendered drafts—and this is particularly true when we are dealing with these male narratives. I did not, for example, look at first for discontinuity or potential in Tim's essay, because he is exactly the kind of student I do not normally read with much empathy or openness: male, aggressive (or passively aggressive), cocky (a word, like *strident,* that carries strong gender connotations), and (not insignificantly) baseball-capped. It is not simply a matter, however, of saying that many of us have trouble with these narratives *and* we have trouble with the students who write them; rather, many of us have trouble with these narratives *because* we have trouble with the male students who write them.

Certainly that was part of the reason I read and listened to Tim's narrative in such an unimaginative way; how else could have I have failed to notice how important this game was to Tim:

> He knew I always went for the candy aisles. What else would I want? Tuna fish? Spam? Jelly beans. Those were my favorite. The trouble was that they tend to make a lot of noise. So they usually ended up down my pants. It was the only place I could put them where they wouldn't move and where Leo could never check. It wasn't very comfortable but it was very efficient. Now I could have gone straight out the door but that was way too easy. First I had to get his attention and get him to follow me. Then I had to lose him and then I would walk out. I was surprised at how many times this worked. It was almost as if he tried to be stupid. How could he not know that I was about to rip him off? Maybe Leo gave me permission. Maybe he didn't want the game to end.

These suggestive references—to what is down Tim's pants, to what Leo could never check, to why Tim almost wanted to get caught, to why Leo almost wanted Tim to get away—seem significant to me now. In retrospect, it all seems so clear to me—Tim is struggling here with his own masculinity, with his relationships with older, powerful men, with his anger at the power that I had as his teacher—that I wonder how or why I failed to see any of that then. Of course, even if I *had* seen all of this at the time, I would not have said so to Tim. After all, it is one thing to tell ourselves that we see more in our students' texts (and lives) than they see themselves; it is another to tell our students about what we take to be their sexual anxieties or dysfunctional family relationships.

Still, if I had been more open to Tim and his essay, I would have read and re-sponded to his essay more generously and imaginatively.

But if he was in some largely unconscious way resisting my authority, then I was in some largely unconscious way resisting his resistance. Normally I would be willing and able to read for discontinuity or, to use my friend Bruce Ballenger's poetic advice, to find the line or passage in the student's text that "dips beneath the surface." That at first I was unwilling or unable to do so—that I was somehow still convinced that Tim's essay was another "typical male narrative"—is significant not only in what it might say about my own resistance but in what it also might suggest about how gender operates in the writing class. For when I reread that essay now, I am struck that though Tim keeps trying to make it a conventional male story about what he takes with him out of the store, he can hardly keep out the suggestions that this essay is really about what he did not have when he entered:

> I remember how much that game meant to me, though I'm still not sure
> I understand why. Every time I walked out of the store with something
> stuffed down my pants or in my pocket, it was the one place I experienced
> victory. It was a win. Rack one up for the angry, young rebellious kid
> with the red hair. I never really thought about what might have happened
> if I got caught or if the game stopped being a game. That would have to
> wait for another round with an authority figure who had a little more
> power than Leo.

Who was that authority figure? And why was the store the *one* place Tim ever experienced victory?

That Tim's essay was turning into something more than he may have originally intended is not surprising; after all, we often think we see more in a student's narrative than the student seems to see. This becomes especially tricky, though, when a student author, like Tim, hints at a problem that he then immediately dismisses or ignores. Or when a student author sums up an unresolved problem in a pat and unconvincing way. For example, after de-scribing a drunken near fatal car wreck in great detail or a summer volun-teering at a homeless shelter, student authors are apt to conclude, "I learned *cliché* never to take life for granted again." Or after writing five pained pages about a mother who always expects the impossible or a father who was never emo-tionally available when needed, we will read, "Sure, my mother is different, she's different in a good way," or, "All I know is how much I love my father." Tim's essay offered an odd version of this "everything is fine" ending: after hinting that his shoplifting may have been connected to deeper, personal prob-lems, particularly problems at home, problems in his relationships with male authority figures, he returns in the final paragraph to the moment at hand and to the odd jocularity he had established in the introduction:

> I rarely saw Leo after I had possession and he had lost sight of me in those mirrors. I could just walk out without even worrying about getting caught. That's good. Rule #355 for shoplifters: don't steal something every time you go into a store especially when they know you are doing it. Rule #356: always, however, look like you had. It's times like that you pray that the clerk accuses you because then you will make them look real bad, piss them off big-time, and give yourself tremendous leeway the next time you walk in that store. If you do all that, you can become a successful shoplifter.

Isn't this what teachers learn?

Tim's attempt to bring the essay back to its lighthearted how-to-shoplift tone makes some sense; after all, that has been a strand throughout the essay and, like many other student writers, Tim is driven by an understanding (or misunderstanding) that every essay needs a neat resolution. Though these "false resolutions" ("My brother's death did teach me to make the most out of every single day") often seem ludicrous, they should not surprise us: many students are not yet ready to deal with the ambiguity or unresolved tension that they themselves have identified, and these pat resolutions may provide them with a means of dealing (or not dealing) with problems that are simply too painful. That is, whenever these problems present themselves, these students rely on long-established coping mechanisms and ego defenses that allow them to complete the narrative (and, perhaps, to fall asleep at night) by telling themselves, "This is really okay."

It is also not surprising that we are never quite sure what to do in these situations. Do we point out the inconsistency between the narrative and its (lack of) interpretation? Do we push the student to deal more fully with the complexity of the issues? Do we take this to be a problem of organization? Of psychological development? While this is always tricky, it is especially complicated when we are dealing with these conventional male narratives, for two reasons. First, blinded by our own conventional reading and response to the sports or delinquency narrative, we may fail even to recognize the seriousness of the conflict that the student has introduced but then quickly dismissed. Second, we may refuse to pay attention to that unresolved conflict because we are afraid that what is beneath the surface will be even worse than what is there on the page. In other words, if the manifest content—a football game, a Halloween prank, a drunken drive—suggests a degree of carelessness, hedonism, violence, or misogyny, what must the latent content look like? We may, therefore, refuse to follow male narratives beneath their surface because we read them intertextually against our worst nightmares of male culture and male violence.

Here, too, I am drawing on my experience as a writing program director who each semester sees dozens of essays that our instructors, for one reason or another, find problematic. Though the bulk of these essays involve matters not directly related to gender (plagiarism or second language problems, for example), there is a small but steady stream of essays each semester written by male students, usually for female teachers, that involve sexually explicit material; many of these also include some threat or even graphic description of violence. While it seems only fair and reasonable to distinguish between a male narrative that reproduces certain cultural codes—about, say, sports, driving, or the value of individual achievement—and a male narrative that seeks to provoke, control, or even threaten its (typically) female subject and female reader, these distinctions are often blurred by our own unconscious associations. Just as my intertextual reading of Tim's essay led me to see it in misleading and reductive ways, here, too, we may too easily connect the dots that separate the somewhat innocent male delinquency essays from the dangerous, misogynist ones.

I do not mean to suggest that this is exclusively or even primarily a problem for female teachers. My own sense is that while many of us make this leap from the traditional adolescent male to the worst incarnations of male violence, we often do so unconsciously. I still remember walking with my then thirteen-year-old daughter through the college town where we live. As we passed a fraternity where a group of shirtless young men in baggy shorts and backwards baseball caps were playing whiffle ball to the loud rap music coming from the speakers in their windows, Lucy said, "I'd like to live in a house like that when I go to college."

I explained that fraternities were only for men and that I disliked fraternities because they still discriminated on the basis of race, religion, sexual preference—though even at the time I said this I had no idea whether I was right. Lucy looked skeptically at me and at the boys on the lawn.

"Do all of them do that?"

"I'm not sure."

"Well, if they don't, I'd like to at least go to one of their parties; they look like they're fun."

"Yeah, it does *look* like fun in a way," I started in response, "but. . . ." And, though it *did* look like fun and though I could clearly see what was attractive about these boys, the next thing I knew I had launched into a lecture about fraternities, drinking, and date rape.

Lucy again dragged me back to facts and evidence. "Did that happen in this fraternity?" I realized that when I read those newspaper stories I never bothered to distinguish between the Greek letters.

She asked again: "*All* fraternities are like that? I can't believe that *all* those boys are like that."

I couldn't either, really, but I was not quite ready to give up the point: it only takes one, I thought glumly.

So What Do We Do?

1. *We should pay more attention to the cultures of adolescent males.*

At first I was reluctant to think along these lines. After all, it is only in the last twenty years or so that we have finally begun to think about the role that women play in the classroom and university. "After two thousand years of concentrating on men," a colleague who teaches women's studies told me, "the last thing we need now is men's studies." It seemed useless to point out that my interest in studying adolescent males and their cultures is really a logical and inevitable outgrowth of women's studies. The problem, as I see it, is that for too many of those two thousand years, too many male scholars acted as if their studies were gender neutral, implying that what they discovered in their research about men applied to women as well. This is precisely why studies of psychological and cognitive development by Freud, Piaget, William Perry, and many others have been rightfully and effectively criticized by feminist scholars. It is also why men's studies scholars argue that research on the construction of masculinity is consistent—rather than competitive—with feminist scholarship. In "A Case for Men's Studies" (1987) Harry Brod explains, "Like women's studies, it too attempts to emasculate patriarchal ideology's masquerade as knowledge. Women's studies explores and corrects the effects on women and our understanding of them—of their exclusion from traditional learning caused by the androcentric elevation of 'man' as male to 'man' as generic human. Men's studies similarly looks into the, as yet, largely unrecognized effects of this fallacy on men and our understanding of them" (264).

By studying the ways that masculinity is constructed for men in the larger culture, we could begin to understand the ways that male students struggle to construct themselves in our classrooms. As Barrie Thorne points out in *Gender Play* (1993), her study of boys and girls in school, this problem of male sexual anxiety begins long before adolescence:

> When asked about the gender situations they find most troubling, teachers and parents of young children often talk about boys. The troubling behaviors lie at opposite ends of a continuum. At one end is the aggressive masculine bonding in evidence when groups of boys disrupt classrooms, derogate girls and invade their play, and make fun of subordinated

"weaker" boys. Boys who engage in this sort of behavior take center stage in many school ethnographies. In fact, as I earlier observed, their style is often equated with masculinity itself. At the other extreme, adults express concern about boys who do not uphold dominant notions of masculinity, who avoid the tough and aggressive, don't like sports, and are therefore vulnerable to ostracism, teasing, and being labeled "sissy," "nerd" and "fag." (167–68)

It is within this context and continuum that our adolescent male students struggle to compose their narratives and their identities. That so many of those narratives are so troubling should not surprise us or tempt us to respond with censure and self-righteousness. But even more important, the fact that so many of these narratives are so unsettling to our students and ourselves should not be used to support the argument that autobiographical writing should be kept out of the curriculum. In fact, the opposite point could be made: since it is so often the central site of conflict, confession, and catharsis, the personal narrative gives us a unique opportunity to help students negotiate the borderlands between home and school, past and present, self and other.

But we will be of little help in this negotiation if we do not know our way around this territory. As feminist theory and scholarship have helped us read the signs and listen to the silences of female voices, narratives, and texts, gender and men's studies could help us to read the "troubling behaviors" and personal narratives of adolescent males. I have in mind, for example, the sort of reading that Susan Glaspell models in her short story "A Jury of Her Peers." In that story, rescued and reinscribed by Annette Kolodny and other feminist critics, Glaspell shows how men read women's texts in limited and limiting ways, oblivious to the nuances and ignorant of the culture that produced them. In Glaspell's story, a group of men fail to solve a murder that has occurred at an isolated farmhouse because they do not know how to read women's texts—in this case, the condition of the kitchen, cooking stove, sewing needles, house pets.

I think that we often make the same mistake when we—male and female academics—try to read the narratives of adolescent males. We often look in the wrong places and miss the central point because we do not know enough about the culture of, say, sports victories, car wrecks, and sexual anxiety in which it is embedded.

Consider, by way of example, the trouble many of us have reading those baseball caps. Now I am not suggesting that all wearers of caps are problematic nor that all problematic students wear caps—only that there is a correlation and intersection of some imperfect kind and that understanding the cap as a problematic text might help us understand our response to these essays and their authors. When I mentioned in that earlier *College English* essay that all of the problematic men in my class wore baseball caps, I intended very little in the way of heavy symbolism. I mentioned it only because it seemed to be a detail that I hoped was somehow symbolic of the status of these male students.

In the intervening years, though, I've noticed a busy intersection between the caps, talk about the caps, the identification of problematic male students, and the resistance of many teachers to male narratives. One of my older, more traditional colleagues has actually included a note on his syllabus—"No baseball caps in class—ever"; another asked the other day in exasperation, "What am I doing—teaching a writing class or coaching a little league team?" Part of the strong response some of us have to these caps is created in part by the complex of contradictory functions the caps serve and by the ways they trigger our resistance to what we take to be the male student's passive resistance while at the same time suggesting the aggression that most of us find problematic in these students. On the one hand, the bill of the cap conceals and protects, sometimes making it difficult to see the student clearly. At the same time, the bill juts out, intrudes, even threatens, not only in its physical sense but also in its reference to cross-racial or cross-class identity. By referring to physical activity (sports or rap music or farm work), to powerful organizations (a professional team, a major university, a rap group, a street gang, a motorcycle manufacturer), the cap allows the wearer to identify and align himself with a power and prestige outside the classroom. Most of all, though, the cap is performative: by wearing the cap during class, the student crosses certain lines of decorum, propriety, and control, and thereby asserts his individuality; ironically, though, since most of his peers are also wearing caps, it at the same time allows him to efface or erase that individuality and to identify with the group. In that sense the male student may wear the cap not so much to individuate or threaten but to connect and conceal.

I need to point out here that the day is long past when the only students wearing caps in class were males. Yet when female students wear baseball caps, as when female students write about winning a big sports game, there may be a certain welcomed degree of originality and code switching that is absent when these acts are performed by male students. When males wear these caps or when they write mock-heroic essays, we may miss the specific gestures and meanings and respond instead to what we dislike in general about male group behavior, about patriarchy, about male violence.

Or about, say, those car-wreck narratives. If we want to learn how to read these celebrations of drunk driving, destructiveness, and self-destructiveness, we need to know more about the experience and consciousness of adolescent males in much the same way that we need as readers of eating-disorder narratives to know more about the experience and consciousness of adolescent females. We can find some of this cultural and psychological information in scholarly journals and some of it, like this paragraph from a revision I recently received, between the lines of the conventional male narratives themselves:

> My parents keep telling me that it is stupid to hang around with some-
> one like Tommy who is always messing around with cars and drugs and
> drinking. I know they're right but that is part of the reason we all like to
> hang around with him. It's weird that when you are doing something
> that could get you killed that's when you feel like you are most alive.

I have also found it helpful to look to feminist literature and research, for it is there that we find the most compelling justification and strategy for reading texts that uninformed readers might find inaccessible, trivial, confusing, or objectionable. Admittedly, there is an irony in borrowing from feminist theory designed to help us hear the voices of silenced women to help us hear the silences behind the voices of aggressive men. But I am not suggesting that we stop trying to hear the silenced voices of women students or that we let these male voices silence others. Nor am I suggesting that we strive to be sympathetic to or supportive of every single essay regardless of its quality or politics. In other words, I am certainly not suggesting that we can or should be sympathetic to and supportive of essays that are misogynist, racist, homophobic, or otherwise objectionable. And while I am on the subject of disclaimers, let me state that I also do not mean to suggest that we should privilege gender above all other factors, including class, race, ethnicity, sexual preference, personal background.

I *am* suggesting that we need to become more informed and open-minded readers of texts—including, in this case, the conventional male narrative—that may at first glance or on initial visceral reaction seem inaccessible, facile, or even objectionable. We need, in other words, to stop reifying our own interpretations of these male narratives, to realize that our readings are often retellings of our own unconscious associations, and to remember that behind every story is another story. What adolescent male students give us in first-draft personal narratives is just the manifest content, the starting point, the conventional story. Our job is to help them to go further by helping them hear what they have not quite said, what is lurking in the background. And if we do not understand that culture or if we find it inherently dull or reprehensible, we will not be of much help in that process.

2. *Since any reading of a student essay is also a rewriting, we need to work harder to sort out the role our own biases and unconscious associations play in our interpretation of and response to any heavily gendered narrative.*

Any heavily gendered narrative is bound to trigger strong personal and un-conscious responses in its reader. In my own case, I have long struggled against conventional male narratives that remind me of males that I competed against during my own adolescence; on the other hand, I have a tendency to over-identify with narratives that are consistent with my own politics, experiences, or philosophy. I am not suggesting, though, that we should (or that we can) keep our own unconscious associations out of our readings and responses. In fact, our own free associations are often our best tools in this process. When, for example, I reread Tim's essay I had two strong associations. First, I sensed that the authority figure with more power that he referred to was his father and that in some significant sense he was trying to write about that relation-ship. Second, I felt that on some level the essay was also about Tim's relation-ship with me. I am not sure how or why I knew that. I suppose that it could have been the description of Leo (I am also dark, short, and ethnic looking) or maybe it was the notebook he carried and the pencil behind his ear. But more likely it was the nature of the relationship, the fact that Tim was trying to get away with something, that Leo was trying to catch him, and that they both were am-bivalent about these roles.

Though both of those associations felt useful to me as a reader, I needed, at the same time, to be careful about imposing them on him as a writer. In our program, we have formed a group of writing teachers and per-sonal counselors who meet occasionally to read narratives of this sort in order to help work out some of these boundary issues—and to try to sort out our issues from theirs. I have been accused, for example, by one of my col-leagues of thinking that *every* male narrative is, finally, a story of Oedipal struggle. "Sometimes," he will argue, "a cigar is really just a cigar. And some-times a story of a Halloween prank is just the story of a Halloween prank." Though my first impulse is to say, "So, Ralph, why are you so threatened by the psychological aspect of these essays?" I need instead to think about how my readings and responses to these kinds of narratives can overdetermine my students' revisions. I need, in other words, to think about how my own experiences—my relationship with my own family, my own sexual orienta-tion, my own construction of masculinity, for example—might help and hinder me as a reader of male narratives.

Though some composition theorists, including Linda Peterson (1991, 175), have suggested that male narratives may give female teachers more trouble while female narratives may be more problematic for male teachers, we found in our group, anyway, that our responses and experiences are more complex and idiosyncratic than that. For example, I did play high school sports so that may be a shared territory with many students (male and female), but the truth is that I have hardly participated in all sorts of conventionally male experiences (those, for example, that have to do with getting drunk, fighting, driving fast, talking with other men about women's bodies, working with my hands, taking it like a man), while I have been included by my wife, my daughters, my mother, and my women friends in all sorts of conventionally female activities. So when I read a male student's narrative of "the night me and my fraternity brothers got drunk and went cow tipping," I am not necessarily any more likely than my female colleagues to share the writer's experience or point of view; then again, I have always felt more comfortable (or less uncomfortable) reading and responding to a student narrative about a messy and painful interpersonal relationship than one about a kayak trip or a trusty dog.

3. *We need to change the pattern of response to these male students.*

My own tendency, when confronted by a male student who seems particularly obnoxious and resistant, is to try not to waste much thought and energy on him—and to remind him and myself that eventually, at grading time, I will be able to get even. Although this response is punitive and unproductive, I have sometimes clung to it in anger and frustration. Recently, though, I found myself on the other end of this man-to-man defensiveness and realized how unpleasant it was to have my own work and person read unsympathetically by a more powerful male. It happened in an unlikely setting: I was on my way to a conference in Britain. As I rushed off the plane to catch my bus, a customs agent stopped me and motioned me over to a side room: "Just a security measure. It shouldn't take long." As I stewed in silence at the customs table, the guard went through first my passport and then my suitcase. I found myself growing increasingly nervous and agitated but, in spite of my irritation, eager to please. "It's an international conference. I've always wanted to visit Wales and, since I'll be presenting a paper, my university in the States agreed to pay my way."

He cut me short with a dismissive wave at my suitcase. "Mind if I look at what's inside your briefcase, then?" he asked as he unzipped it. He began taking out the overheads for my conference presentation. He held up the first one and frowned. "What?" I asked. "Is there a problem?" Still no response. His silent disapproval goaded me on. "This isn't a final paper or anything—but the whole project is being funded by a grant from the federal government." He seemed enormously unimpressed. Which by now was making me angry. I mean who was he to act so haughty, to be so contemptuous of something I had put time into, something I cared about. I wanted to say, "Who the hell are you to be critiquing my work? You're so damn brilliant?" But since he had the power to make things uncomfortable—maybe even miserable—for me, all I said was, "In America there is a lot of interest in these issues. You don't have freshman comp here, but in the States it really is very big." I was on the verge of telling him why the project was so difficult, why I hadn't had time to accomplish what I wanted, what I still might do. But it hardly seemed worth it. He just didn't seem very interested in my work.

This is a long way for me to make you travel to introduce what I want to say about how men teach or fail to teach other men to write. But I can't help thinking that something about the way the customs agent treated me is very much like the way I sometimes treat my male students. I know that many of them resent my authority, resent the fact that I make them show me their work in conferences and class, and resent the way I grudgingly dole out compliments and suggestions. I know that many of them think they are on their way to more important things than I—a comp teacher—am doing with my life. I know that some of them resent the fact that I keep reaching into their private memories and political beliefs. And I know that I sometimes resent their resentment and enjoy my own authority for its power to control.

Though it goes against my first instinct, I find I can be more successful if I encourage these students, if I push myself to find points of identification, and most difficult of all, if I seek to nurture them. Maybe I could begin by unfolding my arms and suspending my sense of judgment. When, for example, I read an essay about male aggression, I often find it difficult to conceal my sense of disgust, let alone find a way to understand and encourage the writer. But if I can be patient enough to withstand the initial angry response many male students have to my authority and the initial angry response I in turn have to their behavior, I often find that a different student and different narrative emerge. Because these students both scare and anger me, I am surprised each time that one suddenly decides to trust me, the class, and himself enough to admit weakness, doubt, vulnerability.

I was not prepared, for example, when Jerry, my most aggressive and least favorite student—the one most apt to challenge my authority in class or to act insensitively toward another student in workshop—brought to his latest conference a narrative about the strange man who showed up at his college dorm room one day, announced that he was his father, explained why he should be forgiven for walking out on Jerry, Jerry's mother, and his familial and financial responsibilities sixteen years before, and then had the nerve to ask, "Don't you think it's time the two of us got a fresh start?" Suddenly it dawned on me that maybe Jerry and I needed a fresh start, too.

Rather than confronting these male students, male teachers may need occasionally to disarm them with empathy. In some sense, this is the corollary to the advice of some feminists, including bell hooks and Susan Jarrett, that female students may benefit more from "an oppositional world view" than from the "safe and nurturing classroom" that most female teachers try to provide (Jarrett 1991, 120). In my own experience, most resistant male students are much less resistant in one-to-one conferences than they are in class. When I met with Tim in conference, for example, and told him what I liked about his writing and how interested I was in his comments about struggling with authority, he began to relax and open up. When I asked him, with curiosity and without judgment, "Why did you always and only steal from Leo?" he said that he did not know but that he was interested in writing more about that. Then to my surprise, in a revision he followed his comment about his troubles with authority figures with a confessional anecdote about an argument with his father that had almost led to a physical beating. The precipitating incident had been his father's refusal to let him wear shorts and a tee shirt to his first day of high school. Tim refused to change; his father refused to back down.

> "Dad, it's pretty hot outside, I think the only way I'll be comfortable is if I go to school like this."
>
> "Tim, I just spent a lot of money on you for new school clothes and you plan to go like this." Danger. We were already setting up a battlefield without giving much attention to peace talks.
>
> "Dad, I really want to wear these to school today. EJ's wearing shorts, why can't I?" I hated to bring my brother into this but I was losing ground fast.
>
> "EJ's been in high school two years. This is your first day. Now march upstairs this second and change into those new clothes."
>
> I didn't even look at him. I had lost him. Come on, Dad, why don't you just say it, fucking say it! What the hell does that mean? He's been in high school two years and THAT'S why he can wear shorts and I can't. That makes sense. Let's see, where can I find that rule, Dad? Oh here it is, Rule #445: One has the privilege of wearing shorts after two years at the school in question.
>
> "I want to wear these clothes."
>
> "I don't care what you want to wear. Do as I say!" And that's when I lost it; as much as I always try to keep my composure and calm, I lost it.
>
> "Fuck you Dad," I screamed.
>
> EJ was horrified. I'll never forget the look on his face as he saw me dash up the stairs with my Dad close behind. I was faster but it didn't matter. There was no place to go. I jumped on my bed. There was some

room to maneuver. He tried to grab me. I pulled away. He swung and missed. I had never seen my Dad raise his hand to anyone.

"Go ahead and hit me. HIT ME! Is that what you want? Do it!" I screamed. He didn't say anything. He stood there, his face stern and un-friendly, almost angry. He walked down the stairs.

I put on those new school clothes over my shorts and walked downstairs past him without saying a word. When I got in the drive-way, I took off the school clothes and left them on his car. I walked to the bus stop in my favorite t-shirt and shorts. That was the way to play the game.

Although I had felt or sensed that there was some connection between Leo and Tim's father, I did not expect that connection to be so direct as the talk about the rules of the game and the "stern and unfriendly" face suggested they were. I was surprised by the depth and complexity this anecdote added to my sense of the narrative—and of Tim. That impression was strengthened still further when I asked him in his next conference if he planned to write more in his essay about the connection between Leo and his father. His response was that he thought that his shoplifting was part of his general rebelliousness and that he would like to try to write about that. But when he handed in his final portfolio, he included this note: "I tried to write more about why I was such a rebellious kid but I couldn't fit it into my shoplifting essay. I did decide to include it in the portfolio, though." And he did:

My parents separated when I was 10 and Dad moved out of the house. The fights and the threats and arguments started long before then so it was no real surprise when they finally decided to call it quits. I rarely saw my Dad after that. It was an awkward situation to say the least. He obvi-ously didn't feel comfortable leaving home. My mom worked as a waitress to support us. That meant that she left for work soon after I got home from school and didn't come home till late at night. It was then that I began to question things. If having a mother and father and family meant that I could count on them and learn and be happy, then how come I didn't have any of that? If learning to be a man meant I needed my fa-ther, then why wasn't he around? If I was supposed to listen to other peo-ple and if I was supposed to be a good little boy, then why did it feel so good when I wasn't?

The thing is my mom moved out of the house when I was in 8th grade. It was a horrible situation. The end result was my father had to come live with us. My brother and I hadn't really experienced much of my Dad after the breakup and then four years later he is our parent. No one ever talked to us. It was just assumed that it would be OK with us for my Dad to move in. We would accept him and he would accept us. It was also assumed that it would be OK for my Mom to move out.

I'm not entirely sure how to fit this into my essay, either. It doesn't have much to do with the ways that I have typically read my male students and their texts. But, like Tim, I think it needs to be included.

5

Fear and Loathing of Fear and Loathing

Analyzing Our Love-Hate Relationship with Emotion

It's the first day of my advanced composition workshop.

At nine A.M. a student just back from a junior-year-abroad program in France reads aloud her essay about how excited she was at first to be in Paris, "that magical place," how worried she was that first week that her French would not be good enough, how homesick she got the next week when she spoke to her family and boyfriend back in New Jersey, how happy she was when her host family took her to Euro Disney, how frustrated she got when. . . .

At ten, a student writer whose entire family—grandfather, parents, cousins, siblings—had all gone to school here at Boston College reads us stories of the wacky, zany experiences that earlier generations of McMullens had at the old alma mater, like the time uncle Tim snuck a pet chicken in his dorm room and the time uncle Ray tricked his roommate by telling him. . . .

In the final workshop of this rather long morning, a student describes in excruciatingly slow and graphic detail three paintings that his roommate has hung on their dorm room wall. "The first portrait is colorful, but not really too colorful while the second one has color, too, but not really that much more color. . . ." The writer wonders why, when these paintings are not particularly beautiful or interesting, anyone would choose to hang them on his walls (at which point his teacher begins to wonder why anyone would choose to write an essay about these paintings). Unfortunately my wondering doesn't stop here. As Jason reads his last page and a half, I wonder by what possible measure these students can be called *advanced* comp students; whether I should go off campus to get lunch at the new Thai place that, I just heard, has a great buffet or whether I should just eat on campus and save the time and money; when, exactly, did I take my last sabbatical—1998? Or was it '99?—and, more important, when, exactly, can I take another one? "Let's see, if it was '98, that would mean that I. . . ." Suddenly I realize that the room is quiet.

"Good, great, thanks, Jason, for reading that. . . . Okay, I want to hear what's working best in this piece so far, where you hear the voice the strongest. But first, I want you to say back to Jason what you hear and see going on in this essay."

"Okay, well, yeah, he's like describing these paintings. The first one is of someone who is turned away and like the second one is someone who is sort of turned away but not completely turned away. And the third one, you can't see his face but you can sort of. . . ."

"So," I think, getting back to my wondering, "if my last sabbatical was in '98. . . ."

My brothers and I are bored, heavy bored. We're home with a teenage babysitter and we've totally run out of things to do, we can't leave the neighborhood, and we've got to include my little brother Jeff. We try baseball, the swing set, building a fort. Nothing captures our interest. Then the idea: if we took all the stuff in the garage—the newspapers, the old blankets and pillows, some old wood, some chairs—and piled it up with those old chairs at the top, it would be like a rocket ship. We climb up the pile to the chairs. The climb is sort of interesting, but once we're on top, we're bored again. Then a second, bigger idea: if we lit a small fire on the bottom of the pile, the whole rocket ship experience would be so much more realistic and exciting. Within a few seconds, the experience was much more realistic and exciting than we ever could have imagined. The flames shot out from under the space ship with incredible speed and heat and then suddenly the whole ship went up in the flames, into one giant ball of fire. My little brother Jeff, excited, starts to count down, "10, 9, 8, 7. . . ."

By then Joe and I are well on our way upstairs to get water and well on our way to imagining our mother's reaction when she pulls into the driveway to see the house burning down. When the babysitter sees us each carrying two glasses of water, she asks, "Hey, what's going on?" "We're thirsty," we improvise, hustling back to the garage. When we open the garage door, we see that the situation there is more spectacularly worse than we ever could have imagined: now the whole ceiling is on fire. Pouring our glasses of water on the spaceship, we grab Jeff by the hand and head back up into the house, this time for buckets, pots, pans of water. "What are you doing now?" the babysitter demands, clearly starting to get suspicious. "We're *real* thirsty," Joe yells over his shoulder. But by now she smells fire. Fearing our mother's reaction almost as much as we do, she grabs a bucket of her own.

Fortunately, a neighbor, who was much more worried about an out-of-control fire than about keeping the whole thing from my mother, has already called the fire department. They pull up around the time my mom does and around the time the babysitter comes running out of the house carrying my baby brother Dan, who has been sleeping this whole time in his bedroom, which as my mother will remind me and Joe for decades to come is right above the garage.

Within minutes the fire is put out, but the spaceship is burned beyond recognition. A fireman calls my brother Joe and me over to the truck where he is holding a big black book: "I want you boys to sign your name in this book. Your names will stay in this book forever. If you never start another fire, no one else will ever know about this one. But if you do start another fire, the fire department will know that you've done if before."

My mother, as upset as I'd ever seen her, turns to Joe and me: "What in the world were you boys thinking?"

A few days after the workshops on the daily life of an American in Paris and the indescribably boring paintings on that student's dorm room wall, I am in a conference with the student who wrote the draft about how his entire family had all gone to Boston College. Everything in the essay seems to suggest that he, too, is taking full advantage of the nonstop hilarity, except for one sentence hidden deep in the last paragraph in which he notes how weird it is that now that he is finally here at BC he sometimes feels lost and isolated.

"How does this fit into what you're trying to say?" I ask, trying not to show too much excitement about what I think is the moment in the essay of greatest tension and potential. "Maybe my revision could be about that?" he says. "I have a lot more to say about that."

In workshop the next week, he brings his revised version, which still includes some zany stories, but now they are presented as his reflections as he sits alone at the back of the church at his grandfather's funeral. Descriptions of his uncles' colorful carnivals and talent shows are juxtaposed with a scene in which he wakes, disoriented, in the middle of a dark night of the soul, to find himself on the couch in the lounge of his dorm, staring at a test signal on the flickering TV screen. Descriptions of his parents' idealized relationship and of their first meeting in a class called Christian Ideas of Love and Marriage are now set against an excruciating scene in which his girlfriend ends their relationship, telling him that she has never been able to trust another man since she was sexually assaulted in her freshmen year. He realizes how out of place and alone he feels—not just at the funeral and at BC, but in his family and in his skin. An uncle claps him on the back: "Dean, you look terrific; how much of that weight have you taken off since you started at BC? Ten, fifteen pounds?" "More like forty," Dean thinks, remembering he hasn't eaten a meal in three days and that maybe he is trying to starve himself to death. "Lately," he concludes, "I wish I could just disappear."

I'm suddenly feeling the same way—wishing that I could just disappear, that is—for as bored as I was with those first drafts, as much as I hoped for something exciting to happen in this class, I now find myself desperately regretting that something *this* exciting has just happened.

What I fear and loathe most about teaching (at least at those moments when nothing seems to be going on in my classes) is boredom and apathy and ordinariness. I think of the students' lack of engagement as proof that I am stuck with the wrong job, with the wrong students. Then I suddenly realize it's proof that they are stuck with the wrong teacher, that I have run out of energy and ideas and confidence. Since I am someone who has always prided myself on being a good teacher, it hits me: I am a fraud as well as a failure.

And so: I assign a provocative writing or reading assignment; I confront the students about the lack of energy in their work; I try to win them over—with charm or food or threats or rewards. And I try to generate some powerful emotion—in their essays; in their relationship to the topics they are reading and writing about; in their relationship with their classmates; and in their relationship with me. But as soon as I am aware that there is what I take to be a powerful emotional quality—in a student essay, in a workshop or discussion, or in my relationship with a student—I start to get scared that the emotion will somehow become difficult to manage or contain and that it will produce hurt or angry feelings in the students who read it, shame in the student who wrote it, or trouble for me for teaching a course that allows such unprofessional displays of emotion when (according to the voices in my head, not to mention the voices in the hallway) I should be focusing exclusively on rigorous critical and textual analysis.

That conference with Dean reminds me once again how something ordinary and mundane can so quickly turn to something extraordinary and profane, such as a suicidal fantasy. Just as my questions may have led Dean to move into riskier territory, the revised version of his essay may be what leads to the radically new direction that the other essays in the workshop now take—a student's description of the day she and her boyfriend found out that he had Hodgkin's, followed by an essay by a woman who was raped after a drinking binge at a party, followed by essays by two different women about fathers who abandoned them (one for criticizing her twenty-two-year-old stepmother and the other one for criticizing her father for failing to show up at any of her middle and high school events), followed by two essays that while claiming to be about childhood memories of summers at the beach were both really dead-grandmother pieces.

As uncomfortable as I felt with the essays that were too dull, that showed too little emotion, I feel uneasy with these in very different ways. Have I coerced or willed or seduced these students into these confessions and powerful displays of emotion? After all, I am the one who felt bored and frustrated that there wasn't enough emotion or tension. I am the one who asked them to read provocative essays such as Judy Ruiz' "Oranges and Sweet Sister Boy" and Lucy Grealy's "Mirrorings." And I am the one who responded in conference and workshop with greater intensity to those essays or even those moments within essays that seemed to generate emotion. Is it because of my teaching style that my students are now producing this flood of emotion?

I've always felt relatively confident that students choose to write confessionally because of their own needs and desires and reasonably confident that I have not coerced anyone into confessions they are not willing or even eager to make. My writing assignments are open-ended and, along with those confessional essays by Ruiz and Grealy, I have assigned humor pieces by David Sedaris, nature writing by Annie Dillard, meditation by Montaigne, political commentary by Gerald Early and Susan Sontag. Still, can it possibly be a coincidence that an entire workshop is suddenly writing about date rape, molestation, eating disorders, abandonment, depression, death? While coercion seems an unfair charge against me, seduction is another matter altogether. I start imagining how the class website of these confessional narratives will look to someone else—my English department colleagues, my department chair, my dean, my students' parents, a critic of expressive writing, that fireman with the black book.

Yes, what *was* I thinking?

It is not a question of whether emotions have a place in the writing class; it is a question of which and whose emotions are encouraged and allowed. Just as we've come to accept that it is either naïve or manipulative to suggest that a classroom or a curriculum can somehow be apolitical (since politics exist whether we acknowledge them or not), we also need to accept that it is impossible to eliminate or even contain all the powerful emotions that are inevitably stirred up in a classroom or in the teacher-student relationship. As much as we may practice the rhetoric of neutrality, objectivity, and professionalism, certain rogue emotions—say, sentimentality or grief or rage—cannot be legislated by simple proclamation. When a student writes, "I am lost. I am lonely. I am about to disappear," a teacher, panicking because this raw emotion makes him feel fear or loathing or both, can decide to focus his response only on "the writing itself" and reply, "You have created an interesting effect here through the repetition of this grammatical structure." However, what that teacher can't do is claim that because he has ignored the emotion, it has gone away or didn't exist in the first place.

"What I fear most," one of the TAs in our program told me the other day, "is not things getting out of control; it's apathy and boredom. I hate that! I hate feeling like my students don't care about my course. And so when I feel that, I shake things up. I do something, anything, to provoke them. That's why I came up with that assignment I was telling you about. It was because my class wasn't going that well. No one was really talking in discussions or workshops. And the essays seemed really flat. So I told them all to write an essay about something they would be willing to die for. They came in with some great stuff—one student who is gay wrote about gay rights; another about defending the country against terrorism; another about racial equality. So then I told them: 'Now you have to write just as passionate an essay taking the opposite position.' I thought it would force them to really think through what they believe in and why they believe it. It would also force them to take into account gaps in their thinking and counterarguments. I thought it was going great: everyone seemed so excited for the first time all semester. But then yesterday, we workshopped essays criticizing homosexuals and blacks, defending the 9/11 bombings. And people started getting really angry and then really upset. What should I do now?"

I file that story behind the similar ones I've heard. The teacher who, frustrated with her students' dry textual analyses, came up with an assignment she almost immediately lived to regret: "Write a letter to me as Arnold Friend," the frightening sexual predator in Joyce Carol Oates' story "Where Are You Going? Where Have You Been?" "And make it as creepy as possible." The teacher who asked her students to read Camille Paglia on the responsibility of victims in date rape cases and then watched in horror when her students got extremely angry and upset. The teacher who allowed (or encouraged?) a student who thought he was writing about his family's love affair with their alma mater to focus instead on his own suicidal fantasies.

Most of us crave a certain degree of emotion in student writers' relationship to their material, in our classroom workshops and discussions, and in our relationships with each student. The problem is that there will be moments—even if we don't push or provoke students—when that emotion will feel excessive or inappropriate to us, when it will pull us out of our role. What is deemed an inappropriate emotion will vary from teacher to teacher, but an essay expressing moral indignation or profound empathy is less likely to destabilize a teacher than an essay expressing great anger or deep despair. In *The Per-*

formance of Self in Student Writing (1997), Thomas Newkirk makes the point that many writing teachers, uncomfortable with the emotion that is produced when a student writes a highly sentimental piece about, say, a loving parent, a lost friendship, or a dead grandmother, fail to recognize the genre. (My original title for this chapter was "Fear and Loathing *of* Las Vegas" because I wanted to build on Newkirk's argument that an intellectual snobbishness about certain expressions of emotion is based on our sense of ourselves as intellectually superior to the kind of people who are susceptible to what we take to be crude or unsophisticated displays of emotion.)

More and more often I find myself thinking how weird and frustrating it must be for a student in this sort of course—encouraged or required to take risks and strong positions, only to see the teacher who did the encouraging or requiring suddenly panic and retreat in the face of strong emotion. It is understandable that we would worry about outbreaks of anger and be afraid they may silence or threaten other students, but it is irresponsible and naïve to pretend that the line between strong opinions and inappropriate expressions of emotion is always crystal clear. For some reason, we expect our students to know—without having to be told—exactly how far they can and should go in a piece of personal writing, even though our ambivalence about emotion and risk taking is written all over the syllabus (if not all over our face).

Until and unless we're able to sort out this ambivalence, we're likely to put our students in awkward and even damaging situations. As bell hooks points out in *Teaching to Transgress* (1994), the privileging of one kind of emotional style and expression over another is actually the privileging of one group or class of students over another. In describing her own experience as an African American student at Stanford University, hooks points out that while "no one ever directly stated the rules that would govern our conduct" in class, it was clear that certain styles of expression were regarded while others were silenced:

> Loudness, anger, emotional outbursts, and even something as seemingly innocent as unrestrained laughter were deemed unacceptable vulgar disruptions of classroom social order. These traits were also associated with being a member of the lower classes. (178)

It seems to me that this same kind of privileging or policing of personal style takes place when without ever directly stating the rules, we respond with embarrassment or anger to what we take to be inappropriate expressions of emotion in student writing. Our response at those moments reveals less about the quality of our students' writing than it does about our own personal styles and unconscious assumptions.

Most of us, I would assume, go into teaching with grandiose fantasies about how we are going to change and shape our students. If we're honest—if I'm honest, at any rate—we want to be one of the teachers who students say changed their life. Another way to put this is that we want to be loved. This, as bell hooks (1994) explains, is a dangerous goal:

> Teachers who love students and are loved by them are still "suspect" in the academy. Some of the suspicion is that the presence of feelings, of passions, may not allow for consideration of each student's merit. But this very notion is based on the false assumption that education is neutral, that there is some even emotional ground we stand on that enables us to treat everyone equally, dispassionately. In reality, special bonds between professors and students have always existed.

And if this weren't risky enough, hooks then goes even further: "To restore passion to the classroom or to excite it in the classrooms where it has never been, professors must find again the place of eros within ourselves and together allow the mind and body to feel and know desire" (199). Now, if you want to stir up some real fear and loathing, imagine talking to your students, your students' parents, or even to yourself about the need in the college classroom for love, desire, Eros.

At some distant college composition conference in New Orleans or St. Louis or New York, I attended a session on the one-to-one conference in which one of the speakers made the point that one-to-one, quasitherapeutic conferences are inexcusable excuses for poorly adjusted, emotionally deprived teachers to try to generate some intensity and intimacy in their bleak little lives. A new convert to conference-based expressivism, I simmered and steamed and sulked. How dare she? Hadn't she read Donald Murray and Muriel Harris? Hadn't she seen the great progress students make in conferences? Did she really think we are so unprofessional as to foreground our own psychological deficits?

Almost twenty years later, I've started to come around to seeing her point (I know that seems a long time but, hey, it took me ten years of therapy to realize that the guy I was mad at wasn't really my high school wrestling coach but my father). I still don't like how cold and critical that speaker sounded about intimacy and relationships, but I'm ready to accept a good part of her argument. There is a danger that our attempts to stir things up, to establish intimate relationships with students, does have a good deal to do with *our* needs. And that is something else to be scared of—that our own emotions will get so stirred up in the stirring up of our students that we will lose perspective and control.

Caught between teaching with too much and too little at stake, we need to find ways to live in the uneasy boundary between too much and too little emotion. Once again, I think it's useful to turn to the model of psychotherapists. Jeffrey Kottler (1993) is critical of therapists who take unnecessary risks: "Certainly it is neither appropriate nor helpful to advocate risky therapeutic interventions to appease some restless spirit in the therapist." But he is equally critical of therapists who "remain basically satisfied with their moderate gains. They will do just enough to get the job done, but not enough to ever produce dramatic results" (154). As dangerous as it is to invite in too much risk and emotion, there is also a cost and different kind of danger in playing it too safe.

As long as I've taught, I've struggled with trying to identify the place along the continuums of tension and emotion where students are most productive as writers. Now I'm thinking more about identifying the place where teachers are most productive as readers. We need to find the tension and emotion in the seemingly dull essay just as we need to find equilibrium in the face of material that could potentially produce fear, loathing, desire. The trick, I am learning, is to stay present but to *do* little. It is a form of teaching best described by Mary Rose O'Reilley (1993):

> Let's assume you are a rather private person. You are not willing to tell your students that your cat died this morning; you do not want to hear about their dead cats. I think, however, that the best kind of teaching comes out of a willingness to stand in one's condition. The best teaching comes not out of dropping your feelings at the classroom door. You don't need to *talk* about being sad or happy; you just need to be present to your own inward life. It's an attitude of mind, a quality of attention. (119)

We need, in other words, to resist our tendency to do too much—to try to take away the student's pain or solve the student's problem—but we need to resist, too, the temptation to shut down the emotion and to dissociate. In other words, we need to resist getting totally swept up in the emotion but we also need to resist our resistance.

My point is that our students' expression of raw or powerful emotions is not inherently good or bad. What matters is what the student is doing with those emotions as a writer and what the teacher is doing with these emotions as a reader. By asking students to look beneath the surface of things, to explore entrenched opinions and values, to examine new perspectives, to write what they don't know about what they know, we are likely to make our teaching more exciting and more meaningful—for us and for them. We are also likely to make it more stressful and even a little dangerous. Staying present, without overreacting, in the face of expressions of trauma or rage or grief can be difficult, frightening, even painful, but that, to my mind, is a good part of what we signed on for.

6

Referring Ourselves to the Counseling Center
Confronting Boredom and Burnout in the Teaching of Writing

I am in my therapist's office—where I have been since sometime in the Reagan administration—and I am talking, again, about being stuck in certain self-destructive patterns. As I list my faults, I sink deeper into discouragement and self-doubt. Will I ever get less neurotic? Will things ever change? And who cares, anyway? I have no real reason to complain: it's not like I'm living in Iraq or Afghanistan; my complaints are all petty, trivial. Getting no response, I begin to describe what's happened since I last was in. Nothing really, I mumble, at least nothing dramatic.

And I begin to tell him a story about how earlier in the week I had had a terrible day. I had gotten up feeling depressed and found that I just couldn't focus on my work. I kept walking from the kitchen to the study to the living room, scanning my cupboards, my hard drive, my CD collection, but finding nothing that really interested me.

By midmorning I had decided that the only way I could get out of my funk was to go out and buy myself a new CD—Van Morrison had just recorded a new album with the Chieftains—and somehow I had it in my mind that that would be the one thing that could lift my spirits. I drove from store to store looking for the new CD but no one had it yet. Feeling even more miserable I decided to try one final place and, to my amazement and joy, they had it! But by the time the clerk handed me the copy, by the time I saw the picture on the case of Van and the Chieftains looking very haggard and middle-aged, with their collars turned up against that cold Irish wind, I started to worry that the CD might not do the trick after all. I told the clerk, thanks anyway, but I don't think I'll take it.

Near the end of the story, I glance up and see—or think I see—a moment of boredom on my therapist's face. I think I see his eyes flicker, on the verge of sleep. This has happened before—and it always jolts me. Sometimes I decide to try harder—I pick up the pace, try to make my stories more pointed and purposeful, colorful and amusing. I sit up from my slump on the couch. I try to make eye contact. I try to be a good student, an interesting conversationalist. But other times his eye flickers make me feel a sudden burst of self-hatred and my voice gets even flatter, my affect even lower, my body slumps still more—and I limp through the rest of the session, holding back, feeling sorry for myself, humiliated and angry that my problems are so dull that even at $130 an hour my therapist has lost interest.

This time, however, I take a different tack. "This therapy is going nowhere," I mutter, "maybe I should quit." I glance up and see that he suddenly seems a little more alert. (This doesn't surprise me: years ago my friend Todd, who like me seems to be a lifer when it comes to therapy, told me, "You want to get their attention? Bring up terminating. They see that open slot in their weekly schedule, the drop in their annual income, and they get desperate.") "I mean, my life is not great," I say to my therapist, "but it's not so bad, either. Everything is really going okay—except for this, that is. I'm just sick of therapy. I mean, *nothing* is happening here, the same old stories by me, same old reactions from you, same old patterns. I'm not having any breakthroughs or epiphanies. I want to be in the kind of therapy where *something happens*. I thought that in therapy the patient was supposed to have some shock of recognition: like that moment when Oedipus finds out the truth." Here he raises his eyebrows. "No! Not *like* Oedipus. I don't want to find *that* out. But something big should be going on here. I know that I don't want to keep complaining about my embarrassingly trivial, boring behavior week after week. I want to get to some great revelation, even if it causes real pain, because that is what I need to clear away all of these years of fog and decay and uncertainty. I want to get to a breakthrough that will lead to some real shock and pain and catharsis. I want to feel cured."

"You're not talking about therapy," he responds, having now regained his equilibrium, "you're talking about opera."

As a writing teacher, I've often been in the therapist's role—I have read far too many student essays that I find dull and listened to too many students offering self-recriminations and regrets about their lack of ability. I have watched students watching me react or not react to their essays, and I have seen the anger directed at me but also at themselves for having even tried. I have seen and heard the humiliation that results from the realization that you have bored someone, even if it is only yourself. Boredom is to some extent self-fulfilling and contagious; a bored person can be boring to teach or be taught by.

I love this quote!

I have often looked out at my unresponsive class of students or sat through a dull day of conferences and cursed my bad luck. Why am I stuck with these dolts? I deserve better. And I think of the mother's line to her son in one of John Berryman's "Dream Songs": "Ever to confess you're bored means you have no inner resources." I think that my students' confession of boredom means that they have no inner resources; but oddly enough I think that my own confession of boredom with teaching says nothing about my lack of inner resources but only confirms my judgment of them—they *are* boring. Of course this is not logical: how can their boredom be a reflection on them while my boredom is not only not a reflection on me but *also* a reflection on them?

I find myself wondering, what causes boredom and burnout in our work? How can we avoid or overcome getting bored and burned out? Or, to go at the problem another way, are boredom and burnout inevitable parts of the process so the task is to find potentially productive uses of our boredom and burnout?

According to most psychologists I've read, boredom and burnout are the result of an inability to modulate the level of tension or intensity in our work. Mihaly Csikszentmihalyi, the author of several books on the subject, suggests that there is a place between boredom and anxiety—the flow state—where we get lost in an activity and become particularly engaged and productive. As writing teachers, though, we are rarely in that flow state: most of the time our work creates a sort of Goldilocks syndrome—everything is either too hot or too cold; in the relationship between teacher and student, reader and writer, the level of tension is either too high or too low.

When one of my classes is not going well or one of my students seem resistant, I often wonder whether there is too much or too little at stake. Have I pushed this student too hard or not enough? There are certainly moments when, wishing for more tension and more drama, I invite my students to take risks, to write about what really matters, to mine family stories, obsessions, and unconscious associations. And the next thing I know the essay my student was writing about the big game turns into an essay about an alcoholic father; the roommate paper turns into a date rape paper; the essay about "The Yellow Wallpaper" morphs into a narrative about the writer's own suicidal fantasies. Like the man who holds up the "SLOW" sign on the road crew, I am someone with a job that seems either repetitive and dull or—if a car fails to slow down or passes by too closely—stressful and dangerous.

Psychodynamic therapies, such as psychoanalysis, are similar to process writing pedagogies in that they recognize the blurry line between boredom and engagement and understand the unboring revelations that seemingly boring details can lead to. In Janet Malcolm's study of psychoanalysis, *Psychoanalysis: The Impossible Profession* (1980), she profiles a New York psychoanalyst, who complains that when he was in training the first patient his supervisors sent him to treat seemed incredibly boring to him:

> I found her in every way disappointing. I had expected a patient who would free-associate, and here they had sent me this banal girl who just blathered. I didn't understand—I was so naïve then—that her blathering *was* free association, that blathering is just what free association is. . . . Only after years of terrible and futile struggle did it dawn on me that if I had just listened—if I had just let her talk, let her blather—things would come out, and that was what would help her, not my pedantic, didactic interpretations. If I could only have learned to shut up! . . . When I finally did learn, I began to see things Freud had described—to actually see for myself symptoms disappearing as the unconscious became conscious. (70–71)

The psychotherapist Jeffrey Kottler suggests in *On Being a Therapist* (1993) that while boredom and burnout may be on the opposite ends of the spectrum of intensity and engagement, they are similar in that both "involve a discrepancy between what one is giving out and what one is receiving" (144). Of course, that raises a crucial question: are we giving out so much and receiving so little because that imbalance is inherent in the material conditions of our work or because we are failing to see the potential for engagement, gratification, collegiality, that exists within our present circumstances? The temptation, of course, is always to blame the conditions—our students, our colleagues, our curriculum, our department's petty politics.

For years, I used to show new TAs in our writing program an essay I had received in my first year of teaching; the essay was a boy's eulogy for his recently and dearly departed dog, Heathcliff. The writer described Heathcliff's cute floppy ears, his rambunctious personality, his adorably naughty antics. Heathcliff, the writer concluded, would always be remembered as a best friend, as an unqualified source of love and support, and as proof, in spite of what the writer's parents had predicted before the family got the dog, that the writer could handle adult responsibilities. I *dare* you to find this essay interesting, I would say to the TAs, certain that they couldn't. But as the years went on, as I finally started to read the essay more empathically and creatively, as I learned to listen to what was not being said, I began to see all sorts of rich layers and symbols in the essay. I saw its heartbreaking poignancy. I saw a powerful Oedipal struggle between an adolescent boy and a controlling father. I even saw (or imagined I saw) sly references to the story of that *other* Heathcliff.

"If burnout is caused by an overload of stimulation," Kottler explains, "then boredom is caused by its absence—at least in terms of subjectively perceived experience" (143). This notion of "subjectively perceived experience" is crucial, for it suggests that the very same work, reading the supposedly boring student essay, for example, could be interesting to someone else—or even to us, on a different day or when we are in a different mind-set.

Where, then, we should ask ourselves and one another, are the boredom and anxiety located? In the student's dull or provocative writing? In our own neuroses triggered by their writing and behavior? In the interaction or dynamic that develops between teacher and student? Part of the boredom, of course, is created by the repetitiveness of our work—we encounter the same kinds of student essays and the same process of invention and revision week after week, year after year—but part is created by our own lack of engagement and creativity. And by our own resistance: "One therapist comments that when she feels bored in therapy it is usually because she wants to cut herself off from issues that are threatening" (Kottler 1993, 152). This feels familiar to me: boredom is not only about the patient or student not being engaging to us; it is also about our effort or need to retreat and distance ourselves from the writing and the writer when something feels threatening. "When a session or a meeting becomes tedious and drags on endlessly," Kottler suggests, "we can look toward ourselves—what are we hiding from inside this cloak of disinterest?" (152).

So What to Do?

1. *Resist complacency; take risks.*

When we are bored with or burned out from an activity, our impulse is to avoid or resist spending more time and energy on it. We don't push ourselves to think about or talk about exactly how and why we are bored or burned out, and therefore we rarely figure out the cause of the boredom or burnout. Immersing ourselves in thinking about the causes and nuances of the boredom or burnout is counterintuitive, but it is precisely that counterintuitive engagement that gives us a way out.

When we are relatively comfortable and secure, there is a disincentive to take risks. Without the risks, though, we stagnate and are more likely to experience repetition, frustration, and boredom. "She would have been a good woman if there was a gun on her all her life," Flannery O'Conner's Misfit says about the hypocritical grandmother who, at gunpoint, suddenly finds Christ and compassion. Similarly, I would be a good writing teacher if someone had a gun on me during every conference, every time I read a paper, every time I prepare a syllabus. But since I've got tenure and no one is watching me very closely at this point in my career, I can keep pushing my writing students and

TAs to take risks while I shrug and decide to use the same syllabus again next year or give almost the same talk with a new title at next year's 4Cs conference.

Many teachers, including bell hooks, have made the point that it is dishonest to insist that our students take risks while we hide behind the security of our jobs and the complacency of our habits. For us, risk taking might have a number of forms: sharing our own autobiographical writing or unpolished drafts with our students; allowing our students to choose the topics and forms of the reading and writing they will do in our courses; choosing texts and topics for discussion that we have not resolved or mastered.

Risks

2. *Confront our own unrealistic expectations about student writing and our own grandiose fantasies about what we can accomplish as writing teachers.*

Here, too, Kottler's advice to therapists (1993) resonates for us as writing teachers:

> Therapists get themselves in trouble with unrealistic expectations and unreasonable goals. No matter what the textbooks and professors say, you are not going to cure schizophrenia by reflecting feelings, and you are not going to wipe out chronic depression by disputing a few irrational beliefs. . . . It takes several years for therapists to realize that some clients will always be the same no matter what you do; and to realize that most of the time you will be underappreciated and overworked. (165)

teachers

The flip side of the crushing disappointment of failing to reach a student is the grandiose fantasy that we can reach everyone we teach or that our teaching will lead to a dramatic breakthrough. While it certainly makes sense to hold our students and ourselves to very high standards, striving for the sort of teacher-student relationships we see in Hollywood fantasies (*Stand and Deliver, Dead Poet's Society, Mr. Holland's Opus,* take your pick) is a prescription for failure, because reality can't possibly measure up to those expectations. Expecting too much is a blueprint for disappointment, cynicism, and, ultimately, boredom and burnout.

3. *Work with colleagues to help sort out these issues and to locate the source of the boredom and burnout.*

Every psychological analysis of burnout identifies working in isolation as the greatest risk factor. Psychotherapists routinely meet in groups to present cases and to seek and give advice about specific patients, but also to give and receive support, reality tests, and empathy. On my campus, we have created a group of teachers who get together to read troubling student essays we have received, to admit confusion and mistakes, and to gain perspective. When we

meet regularly with teachers!

find a student dull, objectionable, provocative, we use this forum to present the case, and often we find that the essay about the unresponsive father or heroic coach or dying grandparent or Don Juan lifestyle has triggered something unconscious in us that is keeping us from working productively with this student. This group helps us to sort out which issues are our students', which are ours, and which are in the dynamic created by our relationship.

(handwritten: Need a little Boredom)

   4. *Finally, and this also seems counterintuitive, we need to accept boredom not only as an inevitable part of the process but also as potentially productive.*

My friend Carolyn told me that when her daughter was young she and her husband forbid her to even use the word—the *b* word, they called it—and felt that Anna's complaint was a criticism of their parenting and another demand—"don't just take care of me, entertain me." This is not unlike the frustration we feel in light of a student's complaint that a reading or a writing assignment or an entire course is boring. Because we are threatened and angered by claims that something in our teaching or in our own personality is boring, we immediately focus on what the charge says about the students who made it, about their apparent lack of inner resources and sense of entitlement.

   But there is another way to look at this. The British psychoanalyst Adam Phillips (1993) makes the point that in our rush to judgment and activity, we miss the opportunity for learning that boredom provides:

> Is it not indeed revealing, what the child's boredom evokes in the adults? Heard as a demand, sometimes as an accusation of failure and disappointment, it is rarely agreed to, simply acknowledged. How often in fact, the child's boredom is met by that most perplexing form of disapproval, the adult's wish to distract him—as though adults have decided that the child's life must be, or be seen to be, endlessly interesting. It is one of the most oppressive demands of adults that the child should be interested, rather than take time to find what interests him. Boredom is integral to the process of taking one's time. While the child's boredom is often recognized as an incapacity, it is usually denied as an opportunity. . . . If the bored child cannot sufficiently hold the mood, or use the adult as an unimpinging auxiliary ego, there is a premature flight from uncertainty, the familiar orgy of promiscuous and disappointing engagements that is also, as it were, a trial action in action, a trying things out. (69–70)

(handwritten left margin: We all need to be able to experience boredom. "find" "take one's time" to "take interests us" what interests us)

Boredom, then, occurs as an alternative to settling too quickly on an idea or activity; in this way, Phillips suggests, boredom works to protect a person while he waits for a discovery or an insight without knowing what that discovery might be or even knowing that he is, in fact, waiting. Seen this way, boredom feel less threatening, less like soul killing and more like soul protecting. In fact, some therapists, including J. D. Sinclair (1982), have argued that boredom "serves to rest the mind and spirit and give them time to rejuvenate" (96). Like REM sleep, Sinclair is suggesting, boredom gives the mind time to process what it has learned and experienced. If this is true, it helps explain why so many first-year students present themselves—in class and in essays—as boring. They are protecting themselves from potential vulnerability and criticism, but they are also retreating into a protective shell as they seek to process everything they are experiencing. "Boredom," Phillips (1993) argues, "is a precarious process in which the child is waiting for something and looking for something, in which hope is being secretly negotiated; and in this sense boredom is akin to free-floating attention. In the muffled, sometimes irritable confusion of boredom the child is reaching to a recurrent state of emptiness out of which his real desire can crystallize" (69).

The trick is not to seek to produce boredom in our teaching (enough of it gets produced in the natural course of things) but rather not to react with defensiveness and desperation when it appears. I know it sounds hokey to say we need to see boredom and burnout not as problems but as opportunities, but I'm convinced that there is something useful we could learn here about our hidden resistance and unrealistic expectations. *Don't be defensive when a student says he's "bored"!*

Let me conclude by going back to what happened with my own therapist and to the ways in which his issues and mine, his boredom and mine, his resistance and mine, are inseparably bound up in our interaction. So which did come first—my boring stories or his bored response? (By the way, Freud used the couch so that it freed both patient *and* analyst from normal interpersonal interactions, such as the requirement to make interested eye-contact; the idea was that both patient and analyst would be freer to do what my therapist did—to zone out, to free-associate, to play with images and feelings that don't necessarily conform to logic or normal discourse.)

However, I am not entirely free of eye contact; I see his eye flickering; and this time I pounce: "Goddammit, what's with you? You find me so boring that $130 an hour isn't enough to make you stay awake?"

He looks embarrassed, so much so that I almost want to apologize: "Forget it; hey, don't worry; my new insurance company is paying a decent percentage these days." But I don't. "It's a fair question," he says, "I was zoning out just then, but not because of you; because of me. Because something you said triggered a painful association for me, and it made me retreat. I messed up. I'm sorry." So now what, I wonder. "So now what?" I ask him.

"Well, I think you'd agree that is not a typical way for me to respond to you—it's an isolated case—but if it weren't isolated, if I did it all the time, you'd have every right to insist that I work on it, here, with you, or at least in front of you. Even though it was atypical, I still was wrong and you have every right to insist that I work on this on my own, so that it doesn't happen again."

"But it's not an isolated case," I say with some hesitation but without any boredom, "you don't do it *often* but I've definitely seen you start to zone out before."

It is an unusual moment in my therapy; suddenly, the session is not about my problems and limitations and slips and unconscious; it's about his—and I imagine that on some level we both crave but fear this role-reversal. But not to worry: the bizarro moment quickly passes and life, or at least therapeutic life, returns to normal.

"Why does my look of boredom make you so upset and angry?" he asks evenly.

I try to stick to what I thought was the point. "Hey, you're the one who was falling asleep at $130 per hour."

But he won't go there again, and soon I am talking about how often I have seen that look on my father's face, about the times over the years that I have tried to interest him and failed and decided that what I was saying was not really all that interesting after all. (Since my father is a psychoanalyst, the lines are blurred beyond even the usual blur most of us have in transference relationships.)

We finish the session by exploring the possibility that my attempt to empty my discussions with him of affect is a resistance to dealing with threatening or painful emotions but also an impulse to re-produce with my therapist my relationship with my father. According to this logic, I tried to bore my therapist to test him, to see if he would be bored, and to see if I would or could confront him on his boredom in a way that I have never quite been able to confront my father. It is certainly true that when I have sensed that my therapist is bored the humiliation and anger have felt familiar. But when I have called him on it, I have a felt an unfamiliar excitement that I can change, that I am changing.

So has my therapy been worth all these years and all this money? And, finally, are there other implications of my therapeutic experience that are useful for all of us as writing teachers? Ah, I'm afraid that we're going to have stop for the moment: our time's about up.

7

Teaching with a Fake ID

A couple of months ago I posted this note on our writing program listserv:

> I'm working on a book chapter called "Teaching with a Fake ID": I'm
> looking at the way that many of us, especially when we first start teach-
> ing, compose a teacherly identity, or more specifically an identity of our-
> selves as readers and respondents to student writing, that emphasizes
> characteristics that are PC, that is, pedagogically correct. We say to our
> students, our colleagues, and maybe even to ourselves that we can read
> any essay by any student and be attentive and focused, knowledgeable
> and intelligent, demanding and caring, fair and objective. I'm calling this
> a "fake ID" because I plan to focus on those "real" moments when we get
> pulled out of the professional identity or role we have composed, when
> we are reading a student's essay and experience un-PC feelings of, say,
> inattention, lack of focus, boredom, ignorance, regression, bias, erotic
> desire.
>
> The reason I'm telling you all this is that I'd be grateful for any feed-
> back: what do you do at those out-of-role moments? I want to argue in
> this chapter that we should acknowledge and even learn to make better
> use of these un-PC emotions and characteristics. Am I losing it?

I hit *send* (with that twinge of anxiety I always get when I post something that
will be read by sixty people) and waited for the responses to roll in. For several days, none did. At first, I worried that by hitting *reply all* I had sent it somewhere else than the listserv—to my dean? to the students in my first-year
composition course?—but after checking that I had in fact sent it to our writing faculty listserv, I developed a new worry: maybe I was the only one of the
staff of sixty who ever had those out-of-role moments. Maybe when I said, what

95

do we do when *we* are reading a student's essay and experience these feelings, maybe *they* were thinking, ignorance? regression? boredom? bias? erotic desire? hey, don't include *me* in your mishegas.

I considered sending out a disclaimer: I don't mean that I *always* feel like a fake and a fraud or that I never act professionally in my role as a teacher; I just mean that occasionally, sometimes, every once in a while. . . . But just then, there was a listserv response from a first-year teacher named Sarah; she said that she had been worried about an interaction with one of her students who was writing an essay that combined research and personal narrative about eating disorders. In a conference in her office, the student had told Sarah that she had been hospitalized for anorexia when she was in high school:

> I began by telling this student about certain works I had read by feminist theorists that really spoke to the heart of her essay: the way women and girls these days are constantly accompanied in their experience by an image of themselves as they are seen by the eye of the other. When a woman stands up in public or walks across an open space, she imagines her appearance from a certain angle, a certain perspective, that is not her own. So she is both subject and object, blah blah, and I suggested to this student that she might rework her narrative to reflect this not only by shifting from moments in the past to the present, which she had already done, but also by shifting from the third person to the first person and thus making her split subjectivity more evident.
>
> But then I found myself describing my own experiences as an adolescent, when I was so thin that the base of my spine protruded through the wall of my stomach, and I was hospitalized with tubes down my throat—and it suddenly struck me that this was entirely inappropriate to share with a student. Not because I feel it in some way too personal, because that was over a decade ago and it now seems like ancient history, but because it revealed a vulnerable part of myself, less authoritative, less directive, less "in charge," less neutral, whatever.
>
> I think that incident did compromise some fundamental distance in the student/teacher relationship. I know that in your writing and faculty development you are always interested in the necessary and delicate tension involved in any interpersonal relationship and communication. It's good, in a way, for my students to see me as human, because if I'm a disembodied head, they won't be interested enough in the class to apply themselves. But they shouldn't see me as too human, or they will perceive me as pure persona rather than intellect, and then they wouldn't respect me (heavens!). There has to be some disparity in our standing; otherwise, mine is not a voice of authority.

An interesting note to the above encounter is that this student now participates far more actively in class discussion and shows a marked increase in interest in the assignments, now that she knows we share the common history of neurotic eating. In that sense maybe it was productive to have overcome the distance implied by decorum, since nothing inappropriate has come of my "stepping out of role." But still, did I compromise my authority in ways that will make it difficult for me to teach and evaluate this student down the line?

In thinking about whom I wanted to be as a teacher, I focused a lot on what was professional and appropriate. But I am aware that in those moments when I most try to take the "appropriate" stance on things, I feel I am being phony, and since I don't coincide with myself in those moments, I find the decorous and distant stance untenable, and my phrases trail off, I seem tentative and halfhearted, and students sense "something weird is going on here." Sometimes my voice actually cracks midword when I'm articulating something I don't really believe. Yikes! Talk about the gap between who we are and who we appear to be—it's like I literally de-subjectify.

What I find particularly perceptive and useful in Sarah's response is that she moves beyond false binary choices. The question is not, as my title might imply, whether we teach as ourselves or as some false sense of imposter, for if identities are composed and performed rather than inherited and simply revealed, then it makes little or no sense to talk about an identity as inherently true or fundamentally fake. But still, as Sarah points out, there are identities that we might have trouble performing effectively because we *experience* them as phony and not consistent in some way with our own sense of self.

This is, of course, a particular problem for new teachers, who are hyperaware of choices they are making—what to be called, what to wear, how to arrange the desks, what tone to take in the syllabus—and often end up resorting to demonstrations of authority that only mystify their students. The writer David Sedaris (2000) describes a disastrous stint as an adjunct instructor in a college writing course:

> Whenever I felt in danger of losing my authority, I would cross the room and either open or close the door. A student needed permission before regulating the temperature or noise level, but I could do so whenever I liked. It was the only activity sure to remind me that I was in charge, and I took full advantage of it. "There he goes again," my students would whisper. "What's up with him and that door?" (86–87)

When I first started teaching writing twenty-five years ago, I figured the only way I could establish some authority was to build my identity as a teacher from the ground up or from the outside in. Like Olivier building a character by starting with the clothes and makeup, I spent hours the night before my first class trying on clothes in front of the mirror and trying to see myself as a competent teacher. I settled that first day on corduroy pants and a tweedy sport coat with a tie pulled almost but not quite up to the unbuttoned top button of a blue work shirt. I was going for the usual ironic, academic look: I wanted to dress formally enough to gain some credibility with my students and supervisors but I wanted to dress informally enough (i.e., the cords, the work shirt, the tie not quite pulled up) so I could keep some credibility with myself. As Libby Rankin argues in *Seeing Yourself as a Teacher* (1994), her study of six first-year TAs, our effectiveness as teachers will depend in large part on our ability to see ourselves as teachers and on the extent to which we can "negotiate some kind of balance between the personal and the professional." If I had not worn a sport coat and tie, my students might not have taken me seriously; if I had worn a nicer sport coat and a tie pulled up tight, *I* might not have been able to take me seriously.

I have had so much trouble with this!

From that first day on, I spent much of my time desperately hoping that I wouldn't be exposed as a fraud. When I taught *The Scarlet Letter,* I read every article I could find so that I wouldn't be humiliated by ever having to say "I don't know" to a direct question. (Sedaris says that he tried to bluff his way "through most challenges with dim memories of the movie or miniseries based upon the book in question, but it was an exhausting exercise and eventually I learned it was easier to simply reply with a question, saying, "I know what Flaubert means to *me,* but what do *you* think of her?" [86].) I kept imagining my students asking me to come up with facts about Hawthorne—his date of birth; previous works; research methods. And I imagined it would be like a scene form *Quiz Show;* everyone leaning forward waiting to see if I was legit. I feared my imminent and inevitable exposure as a fraud and imagined the moment would make Hester Prynne's time on the scaffold look like a picnic. Of course, as it turned out, there were no probing questions about Hawthorne or Hester (in fact, once I got comfortable as a teacher, I would have loved to have students who cared enough to ask hard questions about the course material or my teaching methods).

The truth is that it did not take me long to feel relatively comfortable, relatively like myself, as a discussion leader. But as a reader and grader of student writing, I responded to my fear and insecurity with hypervigilance. I covered students' work in corrections, explanations, and justifications; the fact that I was *the* authority, that I knew more about their essays than they did themselves, was never in doubt and never to be questioned. When it came to grading, I felt I needed to claim a kind of Solomonic wisdom and fairness. I

difference between classroom presence and page presence?

friend vs foe?

told them many times that whether I agreed with their argument or not, whether I liked them personally, would have nothing to do with my assessment of their work. When challenged in any way, I became immediately defensive and even found myself saying things like, "You could give this essay to any English teacher in this school [or maybe I said "any English teacher in the world"] and they would all agree that this is a C+ over B–.""

The gap that existed between who I experienced myself to be as a reader of student work and who I pretended to be when I defended my grades was painfully obvious to me and, I was afraid, to them. No matter how hard I tried to embody the confident, knowledgeable teacher, my insecurity and doubt were always on the verge of leaking through. I knew all too well how hard it was to sustain this tension—between what feels like a fake and a real identity—since my first teaching job was a nearly disastrous stint as a day-care-center teacher. Without any formal training or experience, I had modeled my day-care teaching after my parents' style of child rearing: I was completely indulgent and nondirective, except when the kids did something that disappointed me, in which case I would give my four-year-old students a look that was meant to say, "Why are you behaving so foolishly?" or, if they persisted, "After all the freedom I've given you, why do you feel compelled to disappoint me in this way?"

Of course, none of this worked well with children of that age, who responded to my indulgence as if I had just asked them to act out scenes in *Lord of the Flies* and who ignored my guilt-inducing glances altogether. I came home each night completely exhausted. I knew I had failed to perform the role of a teacher when after eleven months on the job, a girl in my class named Mandy asked me, "Lad, where do you *work*?"

"Here; I work *here*."

"*No*, I mean, where's your *real* job?"

If we think about this as a question of ethos—which, of course, makes sense—then it is reasonable to ask why certain performances of a teaching or reading persona seem either credible or incredible to our students and to ourselves. In his book *The Performance of Self in Student Writing* (1997), Tom Newkirk argues that certain student performances of self are usually privileged in university writing courses over other student performances of self. We tend, he suggests, to prefer performances that emphasize ambiguity, complexity, skepticism, and that make a big deal out of a little thing, like seeing a weasel or pulling on a wet swimming suit, to performances that emphasize certainty, optimism, conviction, and that say the usual thing about a big thing, such as, "I never questioned God till my best friend died." As a corollary to Newkirk's work, I'm wondering what performances of a teacherly self tend to be most effective and preferred.

I've long felt that we teachers too often box ourselves in by trying to live up to idealized roles and by taking on the sanctioned good characteristics of the good teacher, even when those characteristics feel false or inauthentic to us. If a teacher can't successfully integrate a particular technique into his or her overall style, there is little chance that the technique will be effective. Sarah's comment about feeling phony at some points and in sync with herself at others raises questions that go back at least to Plato, Aristotle, and the Sophists: to what extent does it matter if we actually believe in the identity we're trying to perform? While it may be naïve and outdated to argue that we all *have* one stable or real self, it is still the case that some constructions or performances of self *feel* more stable or real to us.

Trying to perform roles that we experience as inauthentic is bound to fail with our students. In fact, trying to embody attitudes or techniques that we believe in but have not yet integrated is also difficult to pull off. Just as David Bartholomae (1985) points out that students' early attempts to incorporate academic discourse are bound to be clumsy, so too are a new teacher's attempts to act objectively, authoritatively, professionally. In my case, I went suddenly from a relatively traditional and directive style—at least as a reader and respondent to student writing—to a radically nondirective teaching style. Having returned to grad school and taken a course with Don Murray, an acknowledged guru of nondirective teaching, I was hooked and returned to my teaching determined to do for my students what Murray had done for me. But in my hands, these strategies were not yet effective and, to co-opt the language of Mel Brooks' *Star Wars* spoof, looked more like the "the Schwartz" than "the force." In other words, I had not yet had enough time or experience to construct a version of myself as a nondirective teacher that made any sense to my students.

Part of the problem was that I was trying to perform a role as a reader that would be impossible for any teacher, experienced or not, to perform effectively. I was under the impression that I needed to hide from my students, colleagues, and even myself the fact that I had not read a lot of books that I thought an English teacher should have read, that I didn't always prepare as conscientiously as I should have for each lecture and discussion, that I feared I wasn't always able to be fair and objective in my assessment of student work. I am not suggesting that the key to effectiveness is full disclosure. There are, in fact, all sorts of reasons for us to withhold our worst character traits. In other words, it is not a good idea to tell students that we find them so irritating or so endearing that we fear we can't objectively respond to their work, to admit that we stayed up late watching TV and only had time to skim their drafts, or to confess that they remind us of our cousin so-and-so whom we've always felt competitive with. Composing a teaching identity is like composing a writerly ethos: we make choices, as Sarah points out, designed to maintain a certain authority, credibility, and identification.

Full disclosure is unrealistic for other reasons, too: the student is not in a position to deal effectively or equally with us around the negotiation of the terms of our relationship. Though Ira Shor and others have suggested interesting ways that we could try to break out of conventional teacher-student roles and power dynamics, the problem still remains that those ways and that negotiation are still occurring within the very power dynamics we are attempting to break down. But while I'm acknowledging the damage we create by telling students *everything*, I am also concerned about the damage caused by revealing almost nothing of what we're actually thinking and feeling. It's one thing to deny or hide most of our out-of-role, unpedagogically correct moments from our students (for full disclosure could clearly hurt them) or from our supervisors (for full disclosure could clearly hurt us), but it's another thing to hide them from our colleagues or even from ourselves. Again I don't mean to set up an either-or choice: acknowledging the existence and potential usefulness of outlawed, unprofessional methods doesn't mean that we are not striving to reach those professional goals of fairness and compassion, rigor and empathy. In fact, I want to argue that we have a *better* chance of being fair, compassionate, rigorous, and empathic if we acknowledge the difficulty of performing those roles and the inevitability that we'll occasionally be unable to operate within them.

Oddly enough, for someone who began building my teaching identity from the outside in, thinking much more about my wardrobe than my mental state, I ended up going very far in the opposite direction. That is, I came to believe in the notion Mary Rose O'Reilley describes in her book *The Peaceable Classroom* (1993) that attention to our inner or inward life would have more to do with determining our effectiveness as writing teachers than any particular technique. For O'Reilley, that meant attending particularly to the role of the spiritual; for me, that meant attending particularly to the role of the unconscious.

That focus on my own unacknowledged motives and responses lead me, first, to recognize how often and how dramatically I failed to live up to the goals and methods I claimed to practice as a reader of student writing. For years I had told my students, my colleagues, and myself that as a reader of their essays I was attentive and conscientious, knowledgeable and intelligent, fair and unbiased. I am not arguing now that these are bad goals or that we should perversely invert them and aim for inattentiveness and lack of concentration, ignorance and lack of intelligence, bias and inconsistency. I am arguing, however, that there are compelling reasons to compose our identities more broadly and in more nuanced ways that allow for the rogue emotions and out-of-role responses inevitably produced when we read and respond to student writing.

1. *Let me start with the case for a strategic or free-floating attentiveness.*

While focus and attentiveness are, of course, necessary at certain points in our reading process and while presenting ourselves as focused and attentive may help us provide an effective ethos—I think of O'Reilley's suggestion that an engaged "presence" is crucial to creating the right classroom atmosphere—the truth is that we often are pulled out of that role. Instead of denying that these moments of inattention exist or simply trying harder to stay alert, we need to pay attention to our lack of attention and think about the potential uses of inattentiveness, free-floating anxiety, and (as I argue in Chapter 6) even boredom.

For one thing, a premature and hypervigilant focus and attentiveness can at certain times be inappropriate, given the task of reading and responding to a very rough draft. I'd propose that a more appropriate response to early draft writing would be a kind of unfocused freereading, a corollary to freewriting, in which we allow ourselves to skim quickly over some sections, free-associate about others. If the writing is not yet clearly formed or focused, our best or only chance of connecting may be at the level of the unconscious. The key to reading certain kinds of student essays—including drafts that are not yet fully clear about intentions and focus—is to allow ourselves to pursue our own free associations. In our effort to be conscientious and careful, we may read too closely and fail to see potential.

2. *The case that I'd make against knowledge and expertise is similar. Too often we think we need to know exactly what a student essay means and need to demonstrate that knowledge immediately.*

While we may, in fact, recognize unconscious or unrealized intentions that our students don't yet see, it is not always helpful to point those interpretations out to the writer. And while it is useful to present ourselves as wise and perceptive readers, pretending always to know more than we do—and more than they do—can reduce the potential for real imagination and insight. In Chapter 3 I make the point that a number of psychoanalysts—Freud, Horney, Jacobs, for example—have suggested that we have a much better chance of finding meaning in inchoate texts when we stop feeling as if we always need to be so smart and so quick.

In fact, this same point has been made a number of times by savvy teachers who recognize the potential pedagogical power in occasionally letting go of mastery and expertise. Daniel Sheridan, for example, argued in a *College English* article (1991) that it can be productive to bring into the classroom texts that we don't know, haven't mastered, and may have less knowledge about than our students. It can be useful for students to see us as readers who struggle, who make meaning in particular ways, who are curious and occasionally confused. Not surprisingly, most arguments for exposing our lack of knowledge to our students usually come from people who are secure in their teacherly role, like Jane Tompkins' suggestion (1990) that we need to let go of our authority and be willing sometimes to make up a course as we go along. The critique that followed—that letting go in this way was easy for Tompkins since she was teaching with tenure at a prestigious university with strong students in small classes—made some sense, but still I wonder if we all couldn't gain more by holding on to less. My sense is that it is often counterproductive for us to struggle so hard as readers of student work to be or to appear intelligent and in control.

3. *Finally, I want to suggest that there may be problems in presenting ourselves as readers who are infinitely objective and fair.*

This issue of fairness comes up particularly in charged and overdetermined situations, such as when we are worried about discrimination based on race or gender or class; when we are worried that we strongly dislike or are sexually attracted to one of our students; when we are worried that other students notice our bias or attraction; etc. In such cases, we understandably seek to control those emotions or at least to control the behavior that such emotions could lead to; however, if we acknowledged these emotions as inevitable, we might find ways to talk about them with colleagues and to make use of them as readers of students and their texts.

What is going here? Why am I repelled or attracted? Susan Jarrett (1991) and bell hooks (1994) have both written about the potential power and usefulness of Eros in teaching. It makes sense that teachers and students who in some abstract way love and desire each other could be especially effective in their roles, as long as this love and desire can be channeled effectively into the work. Maybe the goal is not to try to love and desire nobody in our classes but to find ways to love and desire everybody. Since this is a such a complicated and even dangerous process to think about, let alone *talk* about with colleagues, it requires careful self-analysis and reality testing.

The gap between who we are and who we tell ourselves we are in these cases is the biggest obstacle to our doing our job more effectively. It keeps us from getting training and getting help when we need it. How can we read and respond to student writing when we are inevitably going to occasionally feel anger or rage or boredom or confusion or competition or grandiosity or desire or love or lust? If we refuse to admit that any of those emotions are possible or even inevitable in the writer-reader, student-teacher relationship, then we refuse to figure out how to deal with them.

The problem with using a fake ID is not that you will definitely get caught by the authorities if you use one, but that that you end up wasting a lot of energy worrying that you might.

8

Reading Composition's Misplaced Anxieties About Personal Writing

Don't worry: I'm not about to turn around and adopt a "don't worry, be happy," antianxiety position; I have way too much invested in anxiety—in my personal life as well as my professional one—to turn my back on it now. Having spent most of my career arguing that tension is an inevitable and potentially productive feature of every relationship in the writing classroom, I'd be the last person to argue that we writing teachers have nothing to worry about. A certain degree of anxiety is the inevitable and often appropriate reaction to radically personal writing, and I'm not about to pretend that I don't get provoked and anxious when a student writes about an eating disorder, a date rape, or a suicidal fantasy. But not all of our teacherly worries are equally productive, and I have come to believe that most of our discipline's current concerns about personal writing are misplaced, wrong-headed, and unproductive.

Composition's Misplaced Anxieties About Personal Writing

The anxiety about personal student writing is so deep in the academy these days that it has come to seem almost self-evident: our job is to teach public or academic discourse; personal writing is not public or academic discourse; therefore, teaching personal writing is not part of our job. Never mind that this simplistic syllogism begs or ignores many fundamental and controversial questions about the definitions of academic writing and the parameters of our job. While preparing students to write successfully in their other academic courses is an important aspect of almost all university writing programs, it is certainly not the only possible reasonable goal. "Life is long and college is short," Peter Elbow argued while making the case for a composition course that would

105

prepare students for a wide range of writing aims and activities beyond the university (1991, 136). If we accept the notion that a composition class should not only prepare students for the assignments they will encounter over the next four years but also help them come to see and use writing as a lifelong source of discovery and pleasure, it is not at all self-evident that the teaching of personal narrative is in any way outside our mission.

But even if we were to grant the point that a composition course ought to focus primarily on public, academic, and intellectual writing, that still would not rule out the personal essay. What counts as an appropriate academic topic or form is not fixed and inherent but fluid and culturally constructed. The contemporary interest in personal writing is not exclusively a contemporary interest and, in fact, goes back to the earliest days of writing and writing instruction; while critics of personal writing believe the popularity of this form in contemporary culture and composition classrooms can be attributed to (or blamed on) daytime talk-show hosts such as Jerry Springer, Geraldo Rivera, and Oprah Winfrey, we could just as easily trace the influence to Augustine, Montaigne, Rousseau, Virginia Woolf, E. B. White, or George Orwell. Suggesting that personal writing is inherently nonrigorous and relentlessly narcissistic is a nonrigorous, narcissistic, and, I suspect, disingenuous argument that reflects more of a lack of respect for our students' abilities than for the form itself. In other words, teachers who would acknowledge that personal writing served writers like Montaigne and Woolf well may still be contemptuous of our students' attempt at the form, arguing that eighteen-year-olds lack the talent, wider perspective, and self-awareness to go beyond solipsism. Of course, that same worst-case argument could be used against the teaching of any form, including argument. By acknowledging that our students lack the talent, wider perspective, and self-awareness to argue like, say, Samuel Johnson, Martin Luther King, or Julia Kristeva has and should not lead us to stop teaching argument. In fact, our recognition that our students may struggle to produce first-rate arguments motivates us to make the teaching of this form central.

This same sort of double standard and binary thinking is employed when critics argue that personal writing ignores the larger political and cultural context in which it is produced. In fact, when an adolescent writes about an eating disorder or divorce or date rape, her story is necessarily connected to a larger political and historical reality; to say that the personal is apolitical or necessarily solipsistic naïvely separates personal experience from audience, rhetorical context, purpose, and instruction (which could be aimed at helping the writer see and make clear those larger political and historical implications). This sort of binary opposition also fails to account for the powerful role that confessional narratives often play in public settings, such as the truth-and-reconciliation hearings in South Africa or the congressional hearings in Washington on the link between tobacco and cancer. An effective teacher would push students to see that a personal narrative—or any rhetorical form for that matter—is only one form among many and that there are other kinds of evidence. It makes good sense to ask writers to account for the context of their confessional writing and to identify the public conversations they are hoping to join. For instance, a student writing about the pain of living with an eating disorder or a grandparent with Alzheimer's could constructively be encouraged to research the illness and to consider incorporating some of that research into a hybrid essay. But to flatly assert—in the face of those essays by Montaigne, Woolf, White, and Orwell—that personal or even confessional writing is somehow apolitical or arhetorical is illogical and ahistorical.

I see this same illogic operating when critics suggest that personal writing should be eliminated from the college comp curriculum because "my students already learned it from watching *Jerry Springer*" or "it's all they learned in high school" or "it's a natural form; everyone already knows how to tell stories." In other words, according to these critics, the form itself is too easy, not challenging enough for college students. Of course, everyone grows up playing with words and rhythms and rhymes, but no one would seriously suggest that poetry is not a challenging form for our creative writing students.

In fact, at the same time that we hear that personal writing is too easy for college freshmen, we also hear that it is too difficult for them either because, as Richard Marius argued at 4Cs some years ago, they are too young to have anything original or interesting to say about their personal experiences or because they may come from a family or culture in which self-disclosure is uncommon. The fact that personal writing may be more difficult for some of our students than for others is inevitable, just as it is inevitable that some will have more comfort and expertise than others when it comes to argument, analysis, description, and other forms of academic discourse.

When we craft assignments, it always makes sense to consider our students' needs and limitations but it is a mistake to generalize about whole cultures and even more of a mistake to eliminate forms and genres that we assume are unfamiliar to students of certain cultures; for example, it would be a mistake to assume that all students of a particular background—say, Korean Americans or Native Americans—will suffer in classes that include some personal writing, just as it would be a mistake to assume that all students of some other background—say, Latin Americans or Jewish Americans—will suffer if they *can't* tell stories or write personal narratives. Just as some of our students will be made uncomfortable and self-conscious when asked or allowed to write personal narratives, there are others who will feel equally uncomfortable and self-conscious when asked to write apersonal, academic discourse and middle-class rhetoric. Our policy should not be to rule out rhetorical forms that might make some students uncomfortable but rather to anticipate and be sensitive to this discomfort and to construct assignments, instruction, and a classroom culture that support all of our students as they learn challenging new forms.

That our concern for our students' comfort level, learning style, and previous experience is applied so selectively and inconsistently suggests that our responses to personal writing are overdetermined and that they reveal more about our own discomfort than about any inherent feature of the form. For example, the anxiety that personal writing cannot be graded makes little logical sense. Just as we can establish criteria to evaluate argument, description, cultural critique, textual analysis, and researched writing, we are capable of constructing criteria to evaluate confessional writing. Nancy Mairs (1997), an essayist and book reviewer who often reads and writes confessional essays, points out that "The Literature of Personal Disaster" is just like any other genre in that there are very good and very bad examples. In other words, we ought to be able to tell the difference in quality between, say, a confessional essay by Virginia Woolf and an episode of *Jerry Springer*.

In most cases, when teachers say, "I can't grade personal writing," what they really mean is, "I can tell whether it's good or bad but I am worried that my students will be unable to understand that my judgment is based not on the quality of their experience but on the quality of their writing." While it is possible, even probable, that some students will be upset to receive a lower-than-expected grade on an essay about a very personal topic, it seems a terrible overreaction to rule out an important rhetorical form because it will take us some time and effort to teach and explain. If we are worried that our students might misunderstand the criteria for our grades of their personal writing, then we need to work harder to make those criteria clear. We haven't stopped teaching argument because some students believe that their grades are influenced or even determined by the extent to which their politics and values agree with their teachers'. Designing a composition curriculum only around forms that are easy to assess and not likely to produce conflict is cowardly and irresponsible.

My suspicion is that the grading concern is connected to the larger anxiety about emotion that I discuss in Chapter 5. In other words, there is the anxiety that allowing or encouraging personal writing will stir things up in our students and in ourselves. There is also the fear that this heightened emotion will lead inevitably to a fundamentally unhealthy student-teacher relationship in which the teacher is a voyeur with all the power who has coerced the student, who is the weaker, vulnerable subject, into painful confession. While there is certainly a danger in allowing students to write about what matters most to them, I have never seen or talked to a writing teacher who *requires* students to reveal radically confessional material and then treats that material and student insensitively. To suggest, as some critics have, that direct coercion of that sort is an inevitable or common practice of teachers who assign personal writing is a fantasy that, I suspect, reflects those critics' own discomfort with confessional material. I'm absolutely not denying the danger and likelihood that some students will have difficulty modulating their emotions and will reveal confessional material that will end up causing them discomfort or even shame, just as I would not deny the danger and likelihood that some students in their argumentative writing might reveal political positions or cultural biases that will end up causing them discomfort or even shame. Again, the solution is not to eliminate personal writing or argumentative writing or cultural analysis but to anticipate the risks and concerns associated with these forms of writing and to help students become more capable and versatile writers. To accomplish that goal, we need to pay more attention to the way our unconscious as well as our conscious assumptions may shape our students' writing. As I argued earlier, there is a difference between seduction and coercion, and I will readily acknowledge that students occasionally get seduced into writing confessionally, believing (correctly or not) that radical confession is what their teacher or classmates value most. But here, too, the answer is not to legislate personal writing out of the curriculum but to be more careful about the signals we send our students about our own desires and biases.

It's difficult to sort out these issues in the current composition culture, which seems bent on policing or pathologizing the personal. Even writing teachers who have come to believe that personal writing has a place in their own teaching are often nervous about what someone down the hall or outside the field will think about that decision. There is the concern that our assignments won't look sufficiently rigorous or professional or scholarly, along with the concern that we will appear philosophically and intellectually naïve for teaching in a way that seems to authorize a belief in a unified self, personal voice, and individual identity. I am casting this as a concern about our own embarrassment, self-consciousness, or shame because I'm assuming that on some level, all of us who have taught, read, or tried to write personal narrative know how challenging, rigorous, and valuable the form can be. And so many composition instructors end up censoring themselves not because they think teaching personal narrative is pedagogically suspect but to avoid the censure of colleagues and supervisors who subscribe to less nuanced notions of this genre.

Coupled with our worry that the introduction of personal or confessional writing will look like it requires too little of our students intellectually is the worry that it will look like it requires too much of us psychologically. "We're not trained as therapists" has become a kind of catchall excuse for not allowing personal writing or not engaging students when they reveal personal information. Of course, most of us are also not trained as political speechwriters, cultural historians, anthropologists, philosophers, or media analysts, either, but that seems to give us little pause when we give reading and writing assignments about politics, ethics and values, cultural difference, popular culture. Failing to be therapists, we worry that we might fail to recognize signs that the student is a danger to himself or others. We worry that we might respond inappropriately, causing further damage to the students. And, perhaps the fear underneath these other fears, we worry that we might get sued. All sorts of odd assumptions underwrite these anxieties: that the line between autobiographical writing and psychotherapy is always clear; that someone who shares radically personal material necessarily belongs in therapy; that only trained therapists (and not parents or friends or compassionate fellow human beings) are authorized or qualified to talk with young adults about their fears, pains, even traumas.

While I certainly recognize the differences between writing instruction and psychotherapy, I would argue, as I have throughout the book, that the lines between these two activities are often blurred and overlapping; that we do students a disservice by pathologizing every expression of trauma; that part of our responsibility and opportunity as teachers and responsible adults is to try to help our students bridge the gaps between their personal and academic lives; and that if one of our students is in serious trouble and represents a danger to himself or others, it is actually a good and not a bad thing that the student has brought that information to a responsible and empathic adult.

My Anxieties About Composition's Anxieties About Personal Writing

I worry that the anti–personal narrative argument is just the thin edge of several wedges. Many of the reasons critics use to push personal narrative out of the curriculum (e.g., it's too easy to write, too hard to teach, too hard to grade) are also used to marginalize other forms of creative nonfiction in the composition curriculum. If we focus only on academic discourse in our teaching of writing, what gets left out are exactly the prose forms—description, human-interest pieces, satire and humor, immersion journalism, personal criticism, the meditative essay—that most often get published and actually read in first-rate magazines.

I worry that eliminating or even marginalizing personal writing in the composition curriculum will radically reduce our chance to succeed as writing teachers. I am certainly not arguing that personal writing is the only form we should teach, and I am not denying that students need to learn to use certain features of academic discourse in order to succeed in the academy. But students can become better writers through immersion in the process of writing

and revising in any form, including personal narrative, and the fact remains that students are more likely to immerse themselves in this process if they care deeply about their subject. While it is certainly true that some of our first-year students care deeply or come to care deeply about the academic texts and intellectual issues we choose, it is also true that many of them will work harder and learn more as writers when allowed at some point to write about their own experiences, values, emotions.

I worry that we will fail to see the opportunities to use a student's passion about a personal subject to teach the tropes, conventions, and processes of composition. We need to recognize what should be obvious—that confessional writing raises all the usual rhetorical questions about audience, purpose, point of view, ethos, pathos, logic. We also need to stop assuming that when students write about deeply personal issues they will necessarily be incapable of focusing on craft; many students are *most* willing and eager to search for just the right voice, syntax, and language when they are writing about a subject or from a subject position that really matters to them. Consider, for example, the striking rhetorical sophistication and control of Boston College student Meghan Keaney in writing about her best friend's repeated suicide attempts:

> A while ago I started telling people about her, about it. I never did it for the right reasons, if they are any. I did it to appear interesting. I painted myself in borrowed colors, as the heroic victim. Talked in stoic tones. It worked: people were intrigued by my situation, if intrigue was what I was after. I expected the reaction: people always are attracted to notions of mental dissolution. We are a society that knows our ailments. We categorize them. We honor them. In my short literary history, I've already revisited *The Bell Jar* three times and *Hamlet* four. At the end of each reading I try to determine what exactly it is about breakdowns that is so seductive. I have never completely figured it out, except to say that there is just something alluring about a mind that contains for a while something powerful enough to drive it to its own destruction. Rereading the letter that contained Harper's latest suicide note, I missed her as simply and honestly as anyone has ever missed anyone else. I missed the night swimming in the quarry and the drives along highways, behind abandoned warehouses. I missed how honest she made me. I placed the letter into the box next to the others and began my mental response.

When Meghan submitted the essay, I did feel a need to ask her first, "Is your friend okay now? Are you okay?" but, after a brief and reassuring conversation about that, we ended up talking much more about why she had made certain rhetorical decisions—why, for example, she had chosen to use sentence fragments, why she had chosen to repeat certain words and grammatical structures. As teachers of writing, we can—and should—focus on whether a confessional essay, just like a textual analysis or a persuasive paper, establishes a trustworthy ethos; offers compelling and well-organized illustration; appeals effectively to audience; overcomes the danger of solipsism and self-indulgence; finds the right form and the right language.

By marginalizing or eliminating personal writing, we not only narrow our students' options as writers, we also narrow our vision of our own role and mission as writing teachers. We begin by putting up a wall around confessional material—"I'm not trained as a therapist"—that soon leads to rigid boundaries between our students' academic and personal lives. Too often I hear colleagues say that they immediately refer their students with personal problems to the dean's office or the counseling department, students with housing or roommate problems to the housing office, homesick students to the first-year experience office, students with questions about their future to the career planning and placement office. While there are certainly legitimate reasons for staying on task and for referring students to useful and expert support services, the growing tendency to avoid all questions or problems that are not directly in our narrowly defined job description is disheartening and, since the key to most successful writing is finding hidden connections and integrating seemingly disparate ideas, pedagogically unproductive.

In my experience, there are certain students who will reveal confessional material even when it is not assigned, encouraged, or allowed. The trigger may be an assignment to write a narrative about a personal experience, but it could also be an assignment to produce an argument about affirmative action, an analysis of *Hamlet*, a cultural critique of a Calvin Klein ad. While radically confessional material may be disturbing and may warrant a referral to a counselor or dean, we need to resist the temptation to pathologize too quickly students who confess to pain, anger, shame, regret, depression, violent or suicidal fantasies. I am worried that if we continue to refuse to think about this issue in a sophisticated way, we will respond rigidly, coldly, and ineffectually to the student who intentionally or unintentionally transgresses into confession.

In most cases, confessional writing opens up productive questions for writing teachers and their students to pursue. My anxiety about our field's current anxiety about the radically personal is that it will make our work drearier and drearier as our focus gets narrower and narrower. If Orwell confessed in one of our classes to shooting the elephant because he was afraid of being embarrassed or Ted Hoagland to fantasizing about what it would feel like to push someone onto the subway tracks or Judy Ruiz to trying unsuccessfully to talk her brother out of a sex-change operation, we might be tempted to ask for a rewrite and refer them for counseling. And they'd not be the only ones to suffer. We'd leave out those courageous attempts to get to moments of real honesty and vulnerability and revelation—and our jobs and our lives would be all the poorer for our censorship and prudishness.

If composition teachers marginalize and even outlaw personal and confessional writing, our students may not get any chance within their college education to write about what they take to be important aspects of their life before and outside the academy. Again, I recognize the pressure this puts on us. It is difficult to live with the anxiety that one of our students may have suffered some trauma and may choose to write about it, but it should also be difficult to live with the anxiety that one of our students may have suffered some trauma and may never write or say a word about it to anyone. If the problem a student is struggling with is critical—if, for example, a student has been raped, is starving herself to death, is contemplating suicide—that is all the more reason that some compassionate person in a position of responsibility should know about it.

I also worry that we will make the mistake of thinking that by discouraging confessional writing we will have made our classrooms safe, secure, and anxiety free, that since our students are not writing about painful personal experience, we can comfortably assume that none of them are depressed or scarred or scared. We can congratulate ourselves for having eliminated or reduced the potential for awkward moments, hurt feelings, and disillusionment about grades, all the while ignoring the fact that disillusionment, exploitation, and unhealthy power relationships are as likely to occur when we teach and assign academic discourse as when we allow personal narrative.

Finally, I worry that this backlash against teaching the personal narrative is connected to the backlash against the publication of our own confessional narratives about teaching. Again, I'm certainly not suggesting that autobiographical writing ought to be the only or even the primary form of composition scholarship, but (as I pointed out in the prologue to this book) I am worried and angered by what I think of as an overdetermined, negative reaction to first-person scholarship.

Teaching writing is difficult and anxiety-producing work, and we desperately need to provide the intellectual space and justification for first-person accounts about these difficulties. Instead we seem to be providing intellectual space and justification for those too uncomfortable with their own anxieties and unconscious associations to talk about these issues. While critics of personal writing accuse advocates of the form of bringing their own psychological needs and failings into curriculum decisions, it is often the opponents of personal writing who are imposing their own neuroses on those decisions. Since those teachers are uncomfortable with the sort of intimacy and vulnerability that confessional writing can produce, they make curriculum decisions to avoid it.

My Anxieties About My Anxieties About Composition's Anxieties About Personal Writing

As uncomfortable as I am made by the field's anxieties about confessional writing, I am made even more uncomfortable by my own anxieties about it. Since I am talking about confession, let me be honest: while I can provide professionally acceptable reasons for defending personal writing in the composition curriculum, I worry that my defense of the form is more than a little defensive. The fact is that my commitment to confessional writing is based, at least in part, on some reasons that I'm reluctant to admit or face.

For example, while I've just suggested that the teachers who separate personal writing from all other rhetorical forms are imposing their own unresolved issues about intimacy onto their students and their teaching, I have to entertain the distinct possibility *I* may be the one who is dictating curriculum based on my own psychological needs. Maybe I *do* get a voyeuristic pleasure from reading confessions that are transgressive and, therefore, titillating; maybe I *am* desperate for something exciting to happen in my classes and confessional writing seems an easy way to produce that excitement; maybe I *do* have the grandiose fantasy that I can save my students and that I can make up for the emotionally stingy and unenlightened people they've met up to this point.

The fact that each of these statements rings partly true for me means that I need to keep interrogating myself and my motives. I need to keep examining my own reasons for assigning personal narrative and my own reactions when students do or don't take the opportunity to write confessionally. I think that I'm being honest with myself when I say that I've come to realize lately I am much less interested in reading confessional writing than I was five or ten years ago and much less interested in reading it than, say, human-interest pieces, immersion journalism, or satire. The fact that I keep allowing or encouraging personal writing is now largely motivated, at least consciously, by my sense that some students will greatly benefit as *writers* from being given the chance to write personally or confessionally.

I also worry that I may sometimes promote personal writing too strongly just because some people in my department and my field seem so keen on attacking it. The more I hear the critique that the teaching of personal writing is inherently inappropriate and that the composition curriculum ought to be organized around something more important (which, depending on whom you talk to, could be grammar instruction, academic discourse, cultural studies), the more I'm tempted to push my course even further toward creative nonfiction (you didn't like it when my course included a *little* personal writing; so how do you like *these* apples?). I worry, in other words, that by continuing to emphasize personal writing I am thumbing my nose at those colleagues down the hall or across the country who think I would let them dictate my curriculum any more than they would like or allow me to dictate theirs.

And I worry, too, that maybe I include and encourage personal writing in my courses because I've lost interest in teaching academic discourse, have gotten increasingly bored by it, have grown increasingly bad at reading and teaching it.

Or maybe I cling to personal writing because my father is a psychoanalyst and I am constantly identifying with and competing against him. By allowing students to write about trauma and loss and fantasy and fear, I can make my own work seem important, challenging, and complicated (in other words, I worry, once again, that I'm simply trying to prove that my fifty-minute hours are significant, too). This seems an opportune time to reassert the need for and pedagogical usefulness of self-monitoring and self-analysis. In fact, when I've pushed myself on this topic, I've come to realize that my commitment to personal writing probably has more to with a desire to connect with my mother than with my father, for she was the one who argued for the value of confession, who believed that self-disclosure creates intimacy and growth, and who died before I ever fully acknowledged how much she influenced my thinking on those issues.

Had I world enough and time (not to mention money enough for endless copayments), I'd continue to explore these issues on the page and on the couch. But for the moment, let me just confess that it's taken me twenty years to realize that pedagogical decisions I was sure reflected only careful thought and sound theoretical consideration also reflect my own deeply rooted and largely unconscious biases and allegiances. Now *that* is something worth getting anxious about.

9

What We're Walling In, What We're Walling Out

Reading (and Rewriting) Our Own Bad Assignments

"I'd like to start the workshop with some writing: let's each write down what makes us happy. And then we'll share what we've written."

What I liked about the suggestion was that it was so unlike the dry, academic topics we usually discussed in workshops at academic conferences; what I didn't like was that it made me panic with anxiety. What did he mean by "what makes us happy"? A *professional* thing that makes me happy? A *personal* thing? As soon as I heard the first few responses read aloud, I knew what I had written was inappropriate.

"When I finally solve a difficult writing problem," was the first response. "When I help a struggling student make a breakthrough" was the second. I considered revising or improvising but it was too late; it was suddenly and already my turn. "Something that makes me happy is getting together with people I like and talking about people I don't." Some uncomfortable laughter, but mostly silence. Why, I thought bitterly, hadn't I chosen something professional rather than personal? And if it had to be personal, what was wrong with "spending time with my family" or, to cite Miss Rumphius, "trying to make the world more beautiful"?

There were still ten or fifteen people left to read after my contribution but I could hardly listen. I was stewing about my faux pas. Until Paul Connolly's turn: I snapped to attention when I heard him say that what made him happy was to teach in entirely new and unconventional ways; that lately he'd been thinking about how conservative he had become as a writing teacher; and that he didn't know yet just how he would try to change his teaching but that he enjoyed imagining alternatives. He said he was thinking a lot lately about meditation.

116

"You mean have our students *do* meditation during class time?" someone asked, sounding a little skeptical.

Paul shrugged. "Maybe; why not?"

"But we're not really trained to teach meditation," someone else pointed out.

"And yoga, too," Paul said, talking to himself as much as to any of us, "I'm thinking about doing something with yoga."

"But I think our responsibility is to teach writing, academic writing that will prepare our students—"

"I'm thinking about dance, too."

"In a writing class?"

That Paul's musings seemed outlandish suddenly struck me as outlandish. How had we gotten so stuck and so conservative in our teaching? Why had we—and here I may have only been speaking for myself—gone all Prufrockian in our discipline's middle age, believing that meditation or yoga or dance or even eating a peach could actually seem so daring and risky?

I wondered if Paul meant that we ought to start using meditation and yoga and dance as prompts, methods of invention, heuristics, ways to discover and connect and visualize the writing before getting it down. If that's what he meant, his suggestions didn't seem so radical or unfamiliar; after all, other composition theorists, such as James Moffett (1999) and JoAnn Campbell (1999), have pushed us to think more about the spiritual sites of composing. And many of us have used the sort of zen-inspired prompts from books like Natalie Goldberg's *Writing Down the Bones* (1986); we've use freewriting and brainstorming and collage to help students find their topics. But I sensed that Paul meant something more, that he was suggesting that meditation or yoga or dance could also be alternative forms of production in our courses. Or maybe he was just thinking aloud, wasn't recommending a particular method or approach, but rather wanted to ask questions, play with ideas, search for hidden connections lurking just out of sight.

I think maybe Paul just wanted us to let go—and see where we'd end up. I wasn't sure I was ready or able to do that yet in my teaching. I still felt too worried about what my colleagues or supervisors might say, about how my students' writing would measure up the next semester. Still, I wondered: why was I so reluctant to let go? Why, for example, was I holding on to teaching and assigning forms of writing that generated so little excitement for my students and me? What would it feel like to toss all those tired school forms overboard? I had long ago replaced the compare and contrast exercises, the research papers, the explications *de texte* with persuasive essays, ethnographic studies, and cultural critiques but it still didn't feel as if I were asking students to produce essays in forms they actually wanted to write. What if I told my students that their goal was to delight and instruct their readers? What if I showed them a wide range of nonfiction forms—prose poems, human-interest stories, immersion journalism articles, memoirs, satires—and then asked them: what do you want to write? What if I asked myself: what do I want to read?

The result, I suspect, is that most students would choose to write creative nonfiction rather than school forms and most teachers would begin to look forward to reading their students' essays with anticipation rather than dread. I'm not sure how I—how any of us—got to the point of asking for writing that doesn't fully engage our interest and sensibilities. When I am not being paid to read, I read all sorts of nonfiction texts, including the sports pages, arts section, feature articles, editorials, and letters to the editor in my morning newspaper; all sorts of guilty-pleasure magazines; novels; memoirs; travel writing; listserv threads; literary essays; how-to manuals. In other words, when I am not being paid to read, I read to be delighted or instructed or both at once. At some point I lost my way as a writing teacher and began reading only or primarily to assess whether my students understood what I told them or, more simply, to get through that damn pile of essays on my desk. That kind of reading, as I mentioned in the introduction to this book, is about as delightfully instructive as studying the check in a restaurant when you think the bill couldn't possibly be that high.

Which might be okay, if I believed that I was suffering so that my students might thrive. If I believed that in order to learn to write effectively my students needed to write in school forms, I suppose I could work up the energy to work my way through them. But I've grown increasingly convinced that students learn to write though their own engagement, curiosity, and playfulness. And I don't see much of that in their academic writing. Whenever I've shown first-year students the sort of essays that end up in literary journals or essay collections, they express surprise and envy. Could we write like *that*? Could we write a whole essay that asks rather than answers questions? Or an essay that goes off on flimsy tangents and lengthy digressions? Or an essay, like Judson Mitcham's "The Signature of God" (1996), that jumps from an excruciating narrative about visiting a parent who no longer recognizes her own name to a beautiful description of a flock of birds in flight?

In their book *The Fourth Genre* (1999), Robert Root and Michael Steinberg include six categories of creative nonfiction: memoir, nature essay, personal essay, critical essay, segmented essay (or mosaic), and literary journalism. To some scholars and teachers in composition and rhetoric, these forms—with the notable exception of the critical essay and the possible exception of the personal essay—all seem too literary to be included in first-year writing courses. However, to other scholars and teachers in the field—those most often associated with expressivisim, the process movement, and essay writing—these forms sound only like slightly new names for what we're already doing.

For those of us already teaching personal narrative, descriptive writing, and ethnography, the shift from composition to creative nonfiction might seem at first like little more than a name change. Is there really a significant difference between a course that features, say, nature writing and one that features descriptive writing? Between memoir as it is written, published, and read outside the composition classroom and personal narrative as it is usually taught within it? Could we, in other words, adopt this sexier name—creative nonfiction—for what we want our students to write and what we want to read but pretty much keep the same old curriculum?

I don't think so. It's true that some of the forms of creative nonfiction are already included in many programs—personal writing and critical essays, for example—but some more creative forms are almost never included— segmented (or mosaic or collage) essays, immersion journalism (or new jour- nalism or literary journalism or literary nonfiction), and the meditation. And here, of course, I am thinking of meditation not as a phase of the composing process but rather as an essay form in which the writer thinks through a prob- lem through a series of associations, in the tradition of, say, Montaigne or Didion.

These sorts of literary forms are almost never included because they re- quire a radical change in our thinking not just about our materials and meth- ods but about our whole sense of mission: there are significant differences between teaching first-year composition as creative nonfiction and teaching it as, say, cultural studies, academic discourse, or current traditional rhetoric. First, we can only ask for so many different kinds of writing. As Peter Elbow pointed out in the debate with David Bartholomae about what should be priv- ileged in a composition course—reading or writing—it is easy to say both but in the end, time is limited. In other words, if we include meditation, we might do less textual analysis; if we include some sort of literary journalism, we prob- ably won't do a major, traditional research paper.

But even more than that, teaching first-year composition as creative non- fiction requires a different emphasis and attitude about audience and purpose. You may teach and justify descriptive writing or narrative as a way to teach skills that you might hope or would argue could transfer to academic writing. But nature writing and memoir and new journalism highlight their literary sensibilities, their desire to produce pleasure, their tendency to render rather than analyze. While these are characteristics we look for when we choose books to read, they seem indulgent and irresponsible as the ends of our students' writing.

Ideas!

The tension, as usual, is between product and process. Using collage as a way to generate ideas that will then be neatly organized into an essay is safe and common. Most rhetoric textbooks include all sorts of prewriting processes that then lead to fairly standard, conventional prose forms. Accepting or assigning or teaching segmented (or mosaic) essays as the final result of those processes is much more radical. Similarly, asking students to use research methods that get them out of the classroom and library, maybe off the campus, and into some other part of the world—say, a case study or ethnography—is again very common. Making that search part of the paper—in the tradition of Macrorie's I-search paper—is also not totally new. But making use of the rhetorical strategies of creative nonfiction or new journalism—say, scene-by-scene construction, extended dialogue, or literary language—is still extremely rare in composition courses.

Similarly, most of us are quite comfortable suggesting that thinking through an issue involves nonlinear, digressive, even contradictory steps, but we generally expect those speculative moves and false starts to appear in our students' journals and drafts, not in their final revisions. Our insistence on logic, clarity, straightforwardness, and coherence is well intentioned but in many ways misguided. As Philip Lopate (1989) explains, the opportunity to resist conventional logic and structure is at the center of the essayist's mission:

> While it is true that historically the essay is related to rhetoric, it in fact seeks to persuade more by its delights of literary style than anything else. . . . The essayist must be willing to contradict himself (for which reason the essay is not a legal brief), to digress, even to risk ending up in a terrain very different from the one he embarked on. Particularly in Montaigne's magnificent late essays, free falls that sometimes go on for a hundred pages or more, it is possible for the reader to lose all contact with the ostensible subject, bearings, top, bottom, until there is nothing to do but surrender to this companionable voice, thinking alone in the dark. Eventually one begins to share Montaigne's confidence that "all subjects are linked to one another," which makes any topic, however small or far from the center, equally fertile. (337–38)

We fear these free falls; we wonder how to respond to a form organized by digression, juxtaposition, contradiction, and personal association, let alone grade it.

Again, I am not suggesting that including some forms of creative nonfiction in first-year writing courses is entirely new or radical; while the belletristic tradition no longer occupies the central role it once played, its influence can still be traced in the choice of reading and writing assignments in most composition courses. But, again, to allow students to read an essay by E. B. White or Virginia Woolf and to start off by writing a personal narrative of their own is different than organizing a course around the characteristics, skills, and goals of creative nonfiction.

According to Root and Steinberg (1999), creative nonfiction is marked by these features: personal presence, self-discovery, flexibility of form, veracity, and literary approaches to language (xxiv–xxvii). The problem is that these are exactly the characteristics that make some composition scholars and administrators nervous about the rise (or return) of the belletristic tradition: personal presence and self-discovery raise all the troubling questions—for teachers on the pedagogical right, there is the worry about rigor, standards, objectivity; for those on the pedagogical left, there is the worry about the naïveté of prepostmodern writers who still believe in a coherent, stable self. Flexibility of form is the opposite of what we try to teach when we suggest that there are established tropes and conventions of academic forms that our students must learn and master; veracity seems another old-fashioned bit of foundational thinking that ignores the ways that knowledge is socially constructed; and literary language is almost an afterthought in a curriculum obsessed with clarity, correctness, and academic discourse.

Thirty years after (or into) the process movement, writing teachers still struggle to justify composition courses by connecting them to something else more important: either we are teaching academic discourse and the conventions of grammar and usage that our students can use for their *real* content courses or we are using writing to teach cultural studies or ecocriticism or community service. Emphasizing creative writing in composition courses seems irresponsible to critics on both ends of the spectrum—give them the skills to enter the work force or give them the skills to resist the ways in which they are being written and controlled and manipulated by early-twenty-first-century capitalism. In this debate—give 'em grammar or give 'em Gramsci—inviting students to write to experience and produce pleasure or simply to inform their teachers and themselves seems an anachronism that we cannot afford.

Like many other people in the field, I went from requiring students to write in the modes of discourse—narrative, definition, substantiation, analysis—to trying to move to more hybrid and organic forms of writing, to giving students more freedom and reasonability to chose their own forms. And yet when I look back at my syllabi, the ones I wrote in my modes phase are not as different as I would have thought from the ones I wrote in my postmodes phase. Though Robert Connors perceptively and elegantly traced the adoption and later rejection of teaching according to set forms in his essay "The Rise and Fall of the Modes of Discourse" (1981), what he didn't fully anticipate was the comeback of the modes in only slightly different forms. Years after the modes were said to be out of favor, most writing teachers are still asking for personal narrative, textual analysis, cultural critique, argument about public issues. In other words, they are asking for and reading new essays that look very much like the old essays.

A shift to new forms—let's say confessional writing instead of personal narrative, prose poems and nature writing instead of description, immersion journalism and human-interest pieces instead of the research paper, meditations instead of argumentative essays—might also involve little more than name changes. But in the short run, it would shake things up. The very fact that these forms are not generally recognized and taught in schools would feel excitingly transgressive. After a while, of course, these forms might become as calcified as the old modes of discourse (people, remember, the thesis statements for your rants are due on Tuesday; and don't forget that you need to have your outline okayed before you can get started on your meditation essay), but in the meantime, we might actually look forward to reading what our students write.

When I first started teaching, I was guided by Don Murray's advice. "Make sure the student leaves the conference wanting to keep writing," Don would say. Years later, I amended that wise advice to fit my own style: make sure the student leaves the conference wanting to keep writing *and* the teacher leaves the conference wanting to keep reading that writing. I now see how that same philosophy ought to guide all of our writing assignments; only assign writing projects or forms that our students want to write and that we want to read. The logic here is that just as students need to feel motivated and engaged in order to do their best writing, teachers need to be motivated and engaged in order to do their best reading. If I am tired of reading limp, author-vacated essays comparing Coke and Pepsi or arguing that the drinking age (of alcohol, not of Coke or Pepsi) should be lowered or listing seemingly random facts about whales, cancer, or global warming, then I need to start reading and revising my own assignments.

Doug Hesse, in his essay "The Rise of Literary Nonfiction" (1991), attributes some of that recent rise to motivations that are not entirely pure or noble sounding. Composition teachers, nostalgic for their English-major past and eager to gain some turf or cultural capital, decide to focus on the old-fashioned, belletristic essay. When I first heard this argument, I was defensive, as I usually am when someone makes me think about my own motives and motivations. I was convinced that I had made the literary essay the center of my course for reasons that had nothing to do with my own yearnings or unresolved issues or insecurities.

Now I know better. Our pedagogical decisions are not so pure, nor should they be. We make choices that depend to some extent on our own interests, strengths, biases, and limitations. This doesn't mean that we should ignore the interests, strengths, biases, and limitations of our students, but we teach best when we balance what students want and need and what we are most eager and able to offer. I used to think that it was irresponsible to make such a prominent place for my own pleasure as a reader of student writing. In fact, I used to think that the effort, struggle, and even suffering I experienced each time I read a batch of student essays was a sign that I was doing a responsible job. I can now admit that I teach creative nonfiction and process and conferencing because I love reading and teaching and talking about these forms—personal essays, immersions, meditations, mosaics—much more than I like reading, teaching, and talking about most academic forms. In other words, one of the central reasons that I have moved toward creative nonfiction is that I find it more appealing to work with students on writing that I actually want to read.

But Hesse is right when he suggests that those of us who have finally rediscovered or reclaimed the literary essay in our teaching do so for reasons that are as much political as personal or pedagogical. If we have to do battle with critics who argue that the personal or meditative essay lacks rigor or weight, it's nice to have powerful allies, nice to be able to point out that we are asking our students to write in a tradition practiced by Montaigne, Swift, Emerson, Freud, Woolf, Baldwin, Barthes, Dillard, Anzualda.

This was my plan for this chapter: I would start with a meditation on meditation; move on to a confession on confession; then an immersion on immersion; a rant on rants and—you get the idea. But it was the immersion that got in my way. What I wanted to do was show how and why immersion projects—the sort that writers like Tom Wolfe and Joan Didion and Tracey Kidder have made famous—are viable alternatives to the conventional first-year composition research paper. I considered writing about this issue from inside the head of Drew, a student last semester who over a period of seven weeks spent a number of nights observing a bellhop at the Lenox Hotel in Boston in order to write a night-in-the-life-of piece, or from the point of view of Natalia, who did an immersion piece on a man in Brighton who organizes raves, ecstasy-fueled techno dance nights at abandoned warehouses. That way you would be able to see how it works: what happens when I ask students first to immerse themselves in the research and then, using the techniques of literary journalism—scene-by-scene construction, third-person narration, extended dialogue, literary language, metaphor and symbol—to immerse the reader in the piece.

It was a noble plan, but it didn't work in this chapter for the same reason that it didn't work in my first-year writing class: I just didn't have enough time. "Literary journalists gamble with their time," explains Norman Sims in his book *The Literary Journalists* (1984)."Their writerly impulses lead them toward immersion, toward trying to learn all there is about a subject. The risks are high. Not every young writer can stake two or three years on a writing project that might turn up snake-eyes" (10).

If it takes months or years for an experienced writer to get to the whatness of a thing, how can I ask first-year writers to do it? And if they don't get to that whatness, in fact even if they do, most are very reluctant to use third-person narrative or scene-by-scene construction or symbolism, because these literary techniques demand a confidence or chutzpah that almost none of them yet posses. Or maybe I'm the one who lacks the confidence or chutzpah to stay with this assignment long enough to let it succeed. I know from assigning and reading immersion pieces in my advanced creative nonfiction courses that from this kind of project students can learn more about research and audience, structure, point of view, voice, detail, than in almost any traditional assignment I've ever given. I also know that I've enjoyed reading these more than the critical essays and arguments and textual analyses.

My compromise these days is to ask for human-interest pieces. Short of the full-fledged immersion projects that seem unrealistic in a first-year course, the human-interest piece involves many of the same skills and elements—personal research, interviews, description, narrative. Writing about a LA punk rock band, The Shoegazers, who spend the whole set staring at their feet, a therapist who specializes in the treatment of Holocaust survivors, or a published poet who works as the night clerk in an old Boston hotel, my students produce pieces that are aimed at actual humans who might actually be interested.

I am sick of the assumed centrality of academic discourse. I like what Chris Anderson (1990) says about why he privileges creative nonfiction over academic discourse: "It's the tyranny of bad expository writing that bothers me, and the smugness of that tyranny, the dogmatic insistence on it, and though the essay is only one alternative, it's the one I have the most access to" (248). I think that many of us have turned toward the literary essay and away from expository and academic writing for the same reason. I once heard Don Murray say that he would feel more obligated to teach academic discourse in first-year composition courses if it were not the only thing being taught in every other course that our students take. To paraphrase Frost, before I'd build a wall (in this case, that would be a wall designed to keep rigor and standards and academic discourse inside the composition curriculum), I'd like to know what I was walling out.

I am sick of critiques of nonacademic writing, including critiques of personal narrative and other forms of creative nonfiction, that emphasize composition's service mission to the university. I am long past sick of being asked to define and defend pedagogical choices I've made based on my goals and experience to faculty who know nothing about the field. So here is my new policy: I refuse to listen any longer to criticism from professors in other disciplines who are only interested in the writing program when they want to blame composition instructors for the errors and deficits in logic, language, and grammar that they find in their students' papers. I'll start accepting responsibility for the writing errors committed in other disciplines by my former students as soon as the biology professors start accepting responsibility when a student somewhere on campus gets sick, when philosophy professors have to be on the defensive when one of our student plagiarizes, and when a poli sci professor has to apologize when a student votes for a mean-spirited, right-wing, fundamentalist candidate.

I'm sick of those who act as if creative nonfiction lacks rigor and content and application outside the classroom. I need to be told again how and why a carefully crafted personal narrative or well-researched human-interest piece lacks rigor, content, and application. Why doesn't a eulogy for a grandmother who has recently died involve complex thinking about audience and purpose and tone? Isn't there sufficient rigor in a meditation in which a student wonders why, if there is a God, he would let a childhood friend suffer from a painful and incurable disease?

I suppose what I'm really confessing is that I'm sick of moderation and objectivity. I want someone to stick up for once for excess. What would be so terrible about turning the research paper into a piece of immersion journalism? the argument into a rant? the personal narrative into radical confession? the descriptive essay into a prose poem? The worse that would happen is that there might actually be pleasure and play and passion in our courses.

It seems long past time to start reclaiming the composition curriculum for writers and writing; to treat it more like a fine arts workshop and less like an art history survey; to resist dry, academic writing assignments by allowing and encouraging confessional stories, family stories, literary journalism, humor writing. For those faculty who want to keep teaching and reading school forms, go knock yourselves out. But don't insist that the rest of us join you in agreeing that academic discourse is inherently more rigorous or more useful than more literary forms of nonfiction. After all, think about what Twain accomplished with humor or what Swift accomplished with satire. If we're going to spend some of our time getting together with people we like, to talk about people we don't, those will be the kind of models we'll need most.

more rigorous? more useful?

academic discourse   literary nonfiction

10

Reading Our Classrooms, Writing Our Selves

From "Is There a Text in This Class?" to "Is This Class a Text?"

It wasn't that long ago that most of us in departments of English began asking, "What texts are worth studying?" Just a generation later, our view of our field has shifted so radically that we now are more likely to ask: "What texts are *not* worth studying?" To those of us interested primarily in pedagogy and composition, the initial expansion of the canon seemed liberating and long overdue: if English departments were ready to include texts from previously excluded groups, then perhaps they were ready, too, to take in those of us living on the wrong side of the hierarchical tracks dividing literature and composition, text and nontext, production and consumption. And the subsequent explosion of the "literary" canon—the inclusion in English scholarship of all sorts of extraliterary texts, including movies, paintings, journals, letters, architecture, rap lyrics, advertisements—seemed even more promising: if our field was now open enough to include the reading of signposts and samplers, Madonna videos and Marlboro ads, then surely student essays and teacher stories would finally be seen as texts and artifacts worthy of attention and scholarship.

After years of struggling against the charge that composition was somehow an atheoretical, practitioner's craft, critical theory suddenly seemed on our side. Robert Scholes (1985), for example, exploded the binary oppositions that fuel the literature/composition hierarchy—and we could add the research/teaching hierarchy—and then called for action: "To put it directly, and perhaps as brutally, as possible, we must stop 'teaching literature' and start 'studying texts.' Our rebuilt apparatus must be devoted to textual studies, with the

127

consumption and production of texts thoroughly intermingled" (16). In a similar vein, Terry Eagleton (1983) suggested that departments of English become departments of rhetoric, abandoning the notion that some texts and language are *inherently* more powerful or valuable than other texts and language.

In many ways and in many research-oriented English departments, the vision that theorists such as Eagleton and Scholes outlined has already been achieved. An increasing number of English scholars have moved toward cultural studies and new historicism and away from a celebration of an unquestioned literary, dehistoricized aesthetic. To realize how much has changed in my own department, I need only conduct a quick mental inventory of the current research projects of some of my own colleagues—Tina Turner's autobiography, Madonna's videos, Ayn Rand's novels, Sigmund Freud's dreams, sadistic humor in Freddie Krueger movies, crime reporting in the *Boston Globe,* narratives surrounding the Winchester rifle, human agency in ATMs, Filipino American performance art, the utopian vision of Club Med, eighteenth-century tea service.

And yet in spite of these revolutionary developments, the binary opposition dividing "literature" and "pseudo-nonliterature" that Scholes uses to describe the dismissal of student writing as unworthy of study has hung on. It is hard to imagine any text—a seventeenth-century diary? a '60s sitcom? a B52s video?—that would be seen as having *less* cultural capital and scholarly potential than a student essay. Like many scholars in composition and rhetoric, I have often felt virtually alone in my department in my scholarly interest in student writing, in the literacy narratives of teachers, or in pedagogical theory (a term, I suspect, that is still an oxymoron to many of my colleagues).

I had assumed that the opening up of the materials and methods of our discipline would eventually break down some of the hierarchies and boundaries in our departments; what I underestimated, though, was the depth of resistance in English departments to consider and validate the underlying theoretical questions about pedagogy. In fact, it seems sometimes that English scholars have had to go out of their way *not* to devote their time, attention, and critical theory to their students, their students' essays, their classrooms, and themselves. The result is that teaching (and, I would add, student writing) stands virtually alone as a text *not* worth studying. In fact, as Paul Kameen (1995) has suggested, teaching seems unworthy of even being textualized:

> [But] to presume that the classroom and the figurative roles that we and our students occupy and play out there are either pre- or post-textual constructions, or, even worse, not textual at all, is to fall into the obvious

contradiction with our current critical biases, a contradiction that happens at the moment to allow us to under(deter)mine "teaching" as we construct the preferred versions of "our work," as well as to deploy unselfconsciously an array of pedagogical practices that are directly contrary to our "professed" critical positions. (455)

Driven by departmental politics and traditions, pedagogy continues to be ignored or characterized by many critics and theorists as prosaic, mechanistic, self-evident. And since the same is true of composition studies, those of us who specialize in the teaching of writing are doubly cursed. As Kameen suggests, this bias persists in spite of current theory that suggests there are no limited texts, just limited readings. And, perhaps, limited readers: what are we in composition and pedagogy to make of colleagues who read *everything* as a text—*except* their own classrooms and pedagogical methods? It seems a comically stunning act of denial, like Freud asserting that everything is a phallic symbol—*except* his own cigar.

To many literary critics and theorists, the teaching of teaching presents few compelling questions, offers little mystery or intellectual challenge, and, most damning of all, provides almost no cultural capital. All of which results in the irony that Kameen and Scholes identify: a discipline that has moved in its professed critical positions beyond the reification of certain texts as inherently worthy—or inherently unworthy—of scholarship yet still clings to the notion that pedagogical questions should be kept in schools of education where they belong.

I start with the bias and resistance of many of my colleagues because it is where many of us responsible for teacher training in graduate departments of English *must* start: we need first to overcome the resistance of our graduate students, who often come out of our colleagues' courses to our seminars on teaching with these same biases against scholarship in composition and pedagogy. Almost all graduate students are eager to teach at some point, but very few are initially interested in or even respectful of pedagogy or composition as scholarly and theoretical fields.

An effective program in teacher training, then, needs to identify and address the resistance of graduate students to pedagogical theory and needs to build bridges between the students' previous interests and skills and the ones that they will need to be effective in the classroom. Ironically the materials and methods in composition and pedagogy grow directly out of and into literary studies and critical theory; that is, teaching is a way of reading and writing. Students learn to teach through, first, learning to read the classroom and, second, learning to write themselves within that classroom.

By reading the classroom, I mean that they must learn to read the complex of interpersonal relationships—teacher–student, student–student, teacher–teacher—that shapes all academic work. Of course, graduate students have been observers of these relationships for many years and thus already have started to interpret the classroom. But since their perspective has been as consumers rather than producers of pedagogical theory and practice and since very few teachers attempt to demystify the process of teaching, few graduate students have read the world of the classroom in a systematic way.

By writing themselves, I mean that new teachers must compose teacherly identities through invention, performance, integration, revision, trial and error. In order to make purposeful decisions about specific, concrete issues (e.g., how to arrange the desks in the room, what to wear when they teach, what texts to assign, what grading system to use, and so on), graduate students must first recognize, develop, and invent themselves as teachers.

Teaching as Reading

By suggesting that learning to teach is a matter of learning to read the classroom and write the self, I am presupposing that we are talking here about a certain kind of interactive or dialogic teaching rather than a more traditional model organized around lectures, textbooks, and objective exams. I am presupposing, in other words, that the paradigm in graduate departments of English has shifted away from what Freire (1972) characterized (or satirized) as "the banking method" of education, in which a narrating teacher pours information into passively listening students, and toward a pedagogical approach that among other things is more aware of the critical theory about the indeterminancy of texts and about the ways that subject positions of the students and teachers are culturally, politically, and psychologically situated.

When I suggest that the teaching of teaching is actually the teaching of reading, I have in mind a number of different sites of pedagogical interpretation and response. Perhaps most obvious, we could begin by teaching teachers to read student writing. Too often, new teachers read student essays against very rigid and conservative notions of textuality, looking more for error and deficit than for possibility and potential. Here, too, critical theory often seems forgotten or abandoned, for if texts are created as much by their readers as by their authors and if texts are artifacts that necessarily reveal information about the author's culture and subject position, then why are student essays so often read as if their meanings were determinate and transparent?

As a first step in teacher education, we ought to encourage graduate students to read student essays through the lenses of critical theory; that is, we ought to ask them to read student writing through various critical perspectives—psychoanalytic, feminist, poststructural, new historical, and so on. And since much of the insight and pleasure derived from reading actually occurs in discussions about the text with other readers, we should more often read and discuss student essays with other teachers. The crucial task here is to get new teachers to read these essays as texts to be studied rather than as papers to be marked. Once they begin to overcome their initial impulse to correct, criticize, evaluate, and complain about student writing, they will begin to see that what we get out of any text is directly and proportionately related to what we put into it.

A second step would be to teach graduate students to read their students' texts against their reading of the classroom as a *text.* Just as our discipline has discovered new kinds of texts to read, we have also created new ways to read them. What has yet to happen very often, however, is the application of these ways of reading—for example, feminist, psychoanalytic, cultural, deconstructive—to the materials, methods, and characters of the classroom. In other words, we have not yet fully textualized or theorized our students, ourselves, or our institutions.

Again, this process should not seem as strange as it does to our graduate students, particularly those who have had some experience with semiotics and cultural studies. The problem, however, is that most graduate students fail to recognize the text that we are asking them to read. Much of what happens in the classroom—such as the way a syllabus is constructed or the way the desks are arranged in the room—is so common, conventional, and familiar that it becomes almost invisible to our students. A related problem is that because students are not encouraged to think from a teacher's point of view and therefore are not used to doing so, they are better at evaluating pedagogical decisions than generating them.

We need, therefore, to textualize the classroom through defining and articulating some of the various texts and various readings that grow out of everyday classroom situations. When I was learning to teach, I was most grateful to—and learned the most about teaching from—a graduate professor in American literature who talked through his pedagogical philosophy as he taught. For example, he would say as he passed out a handout, "You might wonder why I walk around the room and give you each the handout rather than giving them to the first person in the row to pass along. Well, I think that the physical gap between the professor and the student can be a difficult one to cross. And here is one relatively comfortable way that I can cross into this neutral territory to establish some connection with each one of you." Or he would say something like, "You might notice that I always start my written comments on your essay or exam with your name and that I always end by signing my name. This ritual of *naming* may seem trivial but here's why I do it. . . ."

He never suggested that we imitate him; instead he suggested that we think about our decisions as teachers in a way that would reflect and generate a particular philosophy, even a particular worldview. In fact, he often went out of his way to point out ways in which our backgrounds and temperaments might lead us to different answers than the ones he had made. By letting us in on his thinking, he was helping us understand the profession we wanted to enter; by demonstrating a way to read the classroom, he was helping us make sense of pedagogical theory. Of course, I could have figured out some of what he told me through observation, but since I was simply not used to looking through a teacher's lenses, there is much that was happening behind the scenes that I never would have deduced. It wasn't just that I didn't yet know the answers about teaching; I didn't even know the questions.

I suppose that an emphasis on this sort of detail, on the nuts and bolts of teaching, might reinforce the notion of our critics that pedagogy concerns itself with necessarily prosaic or pedantic matters. Yet since we seem finally to have agreed that there are not inherently pedantic topics, we need to realize that these topics seem trivial to us only because—to borrow a cliché used to describe the goal of anthropology—we have failed to see the exotic in the familiar and the familiar in the exotic. We have ceased to see, for example, how arbitrary and quirky many of our decisions are. I once surveyed the staff of our creative writing program about how they set up workshops in their classes: Do you start by asking the writer to read the story? Do you distribute photocopies of the story before the class? Do you let the writer speak first? last? at all? and so on. The answers revealed a wide range of methods. But, more interesting, they revealed a lack of recognition of alternatives; each instructor seemed to be proceeding the way she had always proceeded (and presumably the way she had been taught) with very little recognition of the assumptions and implications of (or alternatives to) a particular technique or method.

Operating on the assumption, then, that there is no question about teaching that is inherently trivial or unproductive, I ask my graduate students to think about why some professors stand while others sit, why some students wear baseball caps, how discussion can be shaped by the design of the room or the time of day. I ask them to consider classroom readings such as this one by Mary Rose O'Reilley (1993) on the semiotics of circling: "An architect friend of mine believes that most human problems are, at base, architectural problems. Certainly culture creates spaces that announce a cultural agenda; we can read them like texts. When I went to grammar school we sat in squares of desks bolted to the floor" (40).

What I hope is clear from these examples is that there is rarely a clear line between teacher and student, reading and writing. And so although I have suggested that student teachers need to learn to read the classroom and write themselves, these processes are often actually overlapping and interanimating. I have become acutely aware of the difficulty new teachers have in sorting out these issues and in clarifying their own role and authority within a classroom. Let me try to demonstrate this through an extended example.

One of the new graduate TAs in the program I direct, a twenty-two-year-old master's student named Louisa Alston, came to see me recently with this story. On her first day as a teacher, she had tried something creative:

> After I took the roll and handed out the syllabus, I said, "Okay, now I want you to listen to something"—and I played a tape I made that had two different versions of Eric Clapton's song "Layla." The first is an electric version from a number of years ago, when he was with the group Derek and the Dominoes; the second is that recent acoustic version from his *MTV Unplugged* performance that you hear on the radio all the time now.

Louisa then gave her students a handout that said something like: *Pay attention to the differences between the versions and to the changes that Clapton made. Write about how and why he made those changes and about whether you think those changes are effective.* Louisa said she hoped to make her students notice that Clapton had changed his voice, his pacing, his perspective. She wanted them to see and hear the song in a new way and to see Clapton as a writer making a writer's decisions; she wanted them to see themselves engaged in the same process as Clapton was—inventing, reseeing, revising. And she wanted them to see her as a creative teacher.

As far as she could tell, that first class went great. The students seemed engaged by the two songs, interested in the assignment. She was able to explain the assignment with enthusiasm and, she thought, clarity; she left feeling exhilarated. (In fact, I had happened to bump into her in the hall right after the class and she told me that she "loved teaching.")

It was the *second* class that did her in. She started by dividing the class into small peer groups—three in a group. She then asked them to read their "Layla" responses aloud and to give each other suggestions for revision. Since she wasn't sure what to do during this time—she didn't want to inhibit the peer interactions—she decided to spend a few minutes at her desk reading. But since she was extremely curious about how the assignment had gone and felt awkward sitting at her desk "not teaching," she very soon decided to move around the room. As she stopped to listen to a paper in one group, she heard her name mentioned by a student reading in the next group. "At first

I was going to pretend I didn't hear it," Louisa told me, "or pretend that it was normal for a student to be writing about me—because I didn't want to interfere, especially since it was the very first peer review. But I was really curious what she might be saying about me, so I walked over and said, 'Mind if I listen in?'"

What she heard was a shock: "The essay was a critique of the assignment and of *me*. The student was arguing that as the only African American student in the class she was at a real disadvantage. She said I had assumed that all the students were familiar with Clapton's song—which she said would be a reasonable assumption if all the students were white—but she had never even heard of the song, had never heard of Eric Clapton. But the worst part was the conclusion. She said something like, *Ms. Alston reminds me of all those blond-haired, blue-eyed racist girls at my high school*."

Louisa brought this to me because she wanted help and reassurance. She had not confronted Debra at the time. "I know I should have said something at the time about her attack on me but I was too upset and I didn't want to make it a big deal in front of the other students. But now I'm worried what they think of me for not responding." She wanted to know what she should do now. She wanted to know whether it was too late to go back to that moment, to do it over, to say something like, *The other day, Debra wrote a paper that some of you heard in which she was criticizing me and the assignment for being racist. Let's talk about that.* She wanted to know if I thought the assignment was racist. And she wanted to know if I thought that *she* was racist without ever knowing it.

The problem, though more dramatic than some, gets at the core of what it means to teach teaching. My role was to help this new TA understand what she had done and what she could do in the future; my role, as I have defined it, was to help her learn to read her classroom and to write herself as a teacher within it. But before I could help her write her response, I needed to help her read the text of the classroom. But what is the text here? How do I represent what happened? Is this a story of an insensitive, unicultural, inexperienced teacher? Of a hostile, defensive, manipulative student? Of the volatile situation that grew out of their tension and discomfort with each other? And does this story include the classmates who listened to the student's essay? Does it include me, who, as Louisa's supervisor, was called on to suggest a course of action or reaction?

Where, in other words, does this text stop and start? Any case study of teaching, like any piece of literary nonfiction, has no inherently correct beginning and end. Does the story begin, as Louisa's student might suggest, with Louisa's high school years? And if it does begin there, should it include Louisa's insistence that she wasn't "popular or cool" in high school, that she had never heard of Eric Clapton until recently, either? Or with the student's high school years? With the roots of racism in America? Should the story include the irony that Eric Clapton has spent his whole musical career trying to pay homage to an African American blues tradition that he has managed in some sense to outpace in fame and fortune. Of course, these are not mutually exclusive choices—in fact, they all might very well be true—and, as Louisa's supervisor, I felt my first responsibility was not to tell her the right answer but to help her read this text (or texts) through a variety of lenses and perspectives.

Much like the teaching of writing, the teaching of teaching involves a kind of coauthorship between mentor and student. I could certainly have provided Louisa with a particular course of action—I could have given her a syllabus in the first place that might not have included "Layla"—but I was more interested in helping her develop skills and tools that would be useful to her in other situations and circumstances.

Louisa felt momentarily paralyzed because she couldn't integrate her various readings of the interaction. As much as she wanted to deny it, she worried that Debra might have been correct in suggesting that the assignment had reflected a latent insensitivity or, even more disturbing, a latent racism. At the same time, she wanted to resist Debra's suggestion that the assignment was inherently easy and accessible for every white student and inherently difficult and alienating for every African American. She did not want to "lose" Debra or the other students over this incident, but she also did not want to lose *to* Debra over it. She worried that Debra was challenging her on this issue simply to undermine her authority.

It seemed to me that Louisa had already read this text in insightful and perceptive ways. What she lacked as a teacher was the wider perspective that could help her separate the personal from the political, the latent from the manifest content. A more experienced teacher would certainly have been equally upset by a charge of racism but might also have been able to acknowledge openly to herself and to her students that *every* text—just like every student and every teacher—is culturally and politically situated and that any particular assignment may, in fact, privilege some students over others. A more experienced teacher may have been better able to read Debra and to realize that while her critique of the assignment was perceptive and provocative on many levels, her personal attack on and hostility toward a teacher she barely knew must be a transference of some kind. And finally a more experienced teacher would recognize the threat that Debra might pose to her authority but still might feel secure enough to realize how Debra's insight, resistance, and political activism could still become a productive part of the class.

Teaching as Writing

Though we certainly need to help new teachers make sense of their classrooms, we need to spend at least as much time helping them make sense of themselves. While there is always a performance aspect to teaching, the problem that I see in many new instructors is that they cannot yet integrate who they are outside the classroom with who they are within it. The most serious challenge, then, is to take the materials and methods from their formal training and informal observation and develop a teaching style, personality, self, that seems familiar and integrated.

Too often new teachers merely copy or import technique without developing an overall style and theory that make that technique understandable or effective. We can talk to new teachers about the skills necessary to be a good lecturer or an effective discussion leader. We can describe the elements of a good syllabus or final exam. But that information becomes the basis for effective instruction at the point at which it is integrated into an overall philosophy—that is, at the point at which technique becomes style or, to borrow Annie Dillard's phrase, "sight becomes insight."

According to Erika Lindemann (1995), new teachers generally lack the experience necessary to develop a personal style or philosophy of composition: "Until they develop a conceptual framework to help them sort out what they read and hear, they must teach by trial and error. They must adopt someone else's assumptions until they formulate their own" (3–4). But how does a new teacher develop such a philosophy? Lindemann focuses in her chapters on the knowledge that a writing teacher should have ("What Do Writing Teachers Need to Know About Rhetoric?"; "What Do Writing Teachers Need to Know About Linguistics ?"; "What Do Writing Teachers Need to Know About Cognition?") or on methods they should employ ("Prewriting Techniques;" "Shaping Paragraphs;" "Teaching Paragraphing"). Only in the book's final three paragraphs does she come to this:

> Donald Murray, a writer and teacher I greatly admire, once wrote, "The teacher of writing, first of all, must be a person for whom the student wants to write." To be a person requires honesty and courage. . . . To be a person is much more difficult than being an authority, or a phony, or a mass of sympathies. Yet if we want our students to write well, we must understand what is truly basic to composing—a person communicating with another person. (272–73)

I imagine a new teacher thinking, "two hundred and seventy-two pages of information and methodology and then this final requirement: 'become a person.'" As vague and as overwhelming as this advice might seem, it appears again and again in different forms in different books about teaching. Mary Rose O'Reilley (1993) suggests that above all else a teacher needs a rich "inner life"; bell hooks (1994) suggests that the key is the teacher's own "self actualization"; and Libby Rankin (1994) defines the task simply as "seeing yourself as a teacher."

But with such ambitious and ethereal goals, what should new teachers concentrate on in their training? hooks suggests that "most professors must practice being vulnerable in the classroom, being wholly present in mind, body, and spirit" (21); O'Reilley, who believes that "deep, mindful listening" is at the center of all effective instruction, suggests, "None of us needs an MA in social work in order to listen attentively, but we do need many things we probably don't pay enough attention to: an inner life, a high degree of consciousness and intentionality, good discernment, the love of friends, and grounding in some tradition of values" (51). In *Teaching as a Subversive Activity* (1969), Neil Postman and Charles Weingartner make a number of radical recommendations, including, "Require all teachers to undergo some form of psychotherapy as part of their inservice training" (138), and this:

> *Require each teacher to provide some sort of evidence that he or she has a loving relationship with at least one other human being.* If the teacher can get someone to say, "I love her (or him)," she should get retained. If she can get two people to say it, she should get a raise. Spouses need not be excluded from testifying. (140)

Though there is certainly some degree of facetiousness in this proposal, there is also a measure of seriousness. As Postman and Weingartner go on to ask, do all of the current criteria used for the hiring and promotion of teachers make more sense and offer more guarantee to students than their recommendation that a new teacher be able to demonstrate his or her capacity to participate in a loving relationship?

It seems to me that all of these provocative suggestions—that new teachers be tested for mental health and emotional capacity, assigned to psychotherapy, or sent on Buddhist retreats—grow out of a serious recognition that teachers need to see and in some cases reinvent themselves in new ways in order to be effective in the classroom. They grow out of a recognition that teaching is not only a way of behaving but also, perhaps even more important, a way of being.

What, then, is our role in the development of our students' teacherly identities? Or more specifically, how can we use an English department seminar on teaching to help students develop a way of being? First, it seems to me that we should give graduate students some extended opportunity to talk, think, and write about the assumptions, biases, fears, fantasies, literacies, values, and political beliefs they are bringing with them to their teaching, all of which may ultimately turn out to be more important in their approach than the materials and methods we provide.

Second, we should ask them to do what they are asking their students to do: during the very first week in my seminar on teaching, I ask students to write a draft of an autobiographical narrative. Over the next three weeks, I ask them to discuss this narrative in conferences with me; to revise it several times from different perspectives; to discuss it in peer review groups; to read a section of it aloud to the entire class; to keep a journal about the process of writing and revising it; to "publish" it in a class magazine; and to write about how and why it will influence the ways they teach and read and respond to their students' writing.

I start with this assignment because I want to put my graduate students in the place of their students. I want them to write in ways that feel initially unfamiliar and destabilizing. Since virtually all the writing they are asked to produce in their other graduate courses is not personal or autobiographical or narrative, this assignment stands out as exotic, provocative, exciting, frightening. Another advantage of this assignment is that it begins to help the students think about the construction of a self; as they think about issues of representation and voice and authority in these narratives, they begin to think about those issues in their teaching as well. Finally, since this assignment creates a hyperconsciousness about the roles that the students and I are playing, it allows us to use our seminar as a touchstone for the study of power relationships within the classroom.

Third, we ought to provide models in this process of pedagogical identity making. We can do this initially by asking new teachers to read autobiographical narratives in which the authors focus on how and why they teach as they do. Here are some of the texts of that sort that I have recently assigned: Libby Rankin's *Seeing Yourself as a Teacher;* Wendy Bishop's *Writing Lives;* Richard Murphy's *A Calculus of Intimacy;* Mike Rose's *Lives on the Boundary;* Jane Tompkins' *A Life in School;* bell hooks' *Teaching to Transgress;* Mary Rose O'Reilley's *The Peaceable Classroom;* Robert Brooke's *Writing and Sense of Self: Identity Negotiation in Writing Workshops;* and—so the TAs know what they are getting into—my own *Writing Relationships.*

Finally, and perhaps most important, we can offer ourselves as teaching models. I do not mean to suggest that our pedagogical approach should be held up as exemplary but rather as instructive. In fact, our model will be most useful to new teachers at precisely those moments when we admit to our own doubts and failures. It will be useful because it will liberate them to openly acknowledge their own doubts and failures but also because it will suggest that it is possible to analyze, confront, and control our own limitations. In writing about the influence of the poet Alicia Ostriker on her own poetry and sense of self, Diana Hume George (1994) explains:

> But the most important influence of Ostriker on me is a secret I've not ever committed to paper. It's about being afraid, really scared, of one's own hard selfishness and spiritual smallness. It's about being afraid of your fear. Mentors, as a class, always seem unafraid. Their mothers or mates or brothers or friends may know that they are, but not their understudies. Alicia has never hesitated to tell me how pockmarked her soul can be, how astonished she is at her own mental cruelties, how disappointed in her selfishness. . . . She is fearless about facing her fear. (51)

Though George is writing about a writing mentor, her comments are relevant to us in our work as teaching mentors. Much of our emphasis has to be on demystifying our profession and demystifying ourselves. By allowing our students to see the inevitable gaps between our theoretical goals and practical achievements, we give them the courage to take risks in their own classrooms and a realistic model to follow when they begin writing themselves as teachers.

Works Cited

Anderson, Chris. 1990. "Late Night Thoughts on Writing and Teaching Essays." In *The Fourth Genre: Contemporary Writers of/on Creative Nonfiction,* edited by Robert Root Jr. and Michael Steinberg. Boston: Allyn and Bacon, 1999.

B. D. 1994. "Flow." In *Fresh Ink: Essays from Boston College's First-Year Writing Seminar.* Vol. 1. 39–40. Chestnut Hill, MA: Boston College Press.

Bartholomae, David. 1985. "Inventing the University." In *When a Writer Can't Write: Studies in Writer's Block and Other Composing Process Problems,* edited by Mike Rose. New York and London: Guilford.

Berentson, Jan, ed. 1994. *Dressing for Dinner in the Naked City and Other Tales from the Wall Street Journal's Middle Column.* New York: Hyperion.

Berryman, John. 1969. "Dream Song 14." In *The Dream Songs.* New York: Farrar, Straus and Giroux.

Brod, Harry. 1987. "A Case for Men's Studies." In *Changing Men: New Directions in Research on Men and Masculinity,* edited by Michael S. Kimmel, 263–77. Newbury Park, CA: Sage.

Brooke, Robert. 1991. *Writing and Sense of Self: Identity Negotiation in Writing Workshops.* Urbana, IL: NCTE.

Campbell, JoAnn. 1999. "Writing to Heal: Using Meditation in the Writing Process." In *Writing, Teaching, Learning: A Sourcebook,* edited by Richard L. Graves, 303–6. Portsmouth, NH: Heinemann Boynton/Cook.

Case, Sue-Ellen. 1989. "Toward a Butch-Femme Aesthetic." In *Making a Spectacle: Feminist Essays on Contemporary Women's Theatre,* edited by Lynda Hart, 282–99. Ann Arbor: University of Michigan Press.

Connors, Robert J. 1981. "The Rise and Fall of the Modes of Discourse." *College Composition and Communication* 32: 444–63.

Csikszentmihalyi, Mihaly. 1990. *Flow: The Psychology of Optimal Experience.* New York: HarperCollins.

Fish, Stanley. 1980. "How to Recognize a Poem When You See One." In *Is There a Text in This Class? The Authorities of Interpretitive Communities.* Cambridge: Harvard University Press.

Eagleton, Terry. 1983. *Literary Theory: An Introduction.* Minneapolis: University of Minnesota Press.

Elbow, Peter. 1991. "Reflections on Academic Discourse: How It Relates to Freshmen and Colleagues." *College English* 53 (2): 135–55.

Emig, Janet. 1983. "The Uses of the Unconscious in Composing." In *The Web of Meaning: Essays on Writing, Teaching, Learning, and Thinking.* Portsmouth, NH: Heinemann Boynton/Cook.

Flynn, Elizabeth A. 1988. "Composing as a Woman." *College Composition and Communication* 39 (December): 423–35.

Freire, Paulo. 1972. *Pedagogy of the Oppressed.* New York: Herder.

Freud, Sigmund. 1912. *Recommendations to Physicians Practicing Psychoanalysis.* Stand. ed. Vol. 12, 111–20. London: Hogarth, 1958.

Ganguly, Keya. 1992. "Migrant Identities: Personal Memory and Construction of Selfhood." *Cultural Studies* 6 (1): 27–50.

George, Diana Hume. 1994. "A Vision of My Obscured Soul." *The Ohio Review* 51 (special-feature issue: *Mentors: Essays by Contemporary Writers*): 41–52.

Goldberg, Natalie. 1986. *Writing Down the Bones: Freeing the Writer Within.* Boston: Shambhala.

Hesse, Douglas. 1991. "The Rise of Literary Nonfiction: A Cautionary Assay." *The Journal of Advanced Composition* 11 (2): 323–33.

hooks, bell. 1994. "Eros, Eroticism, and the Pedagogical Process." In *Teaching to Transgress: Education as the Practice of Freedom,* 191–200. New York: Routledge.

Horney, Karen. 1999. *The Therapeutic Process: Essays and Lecture,* edited by Bernard Paris. New Haven: Yale University Press.

Jacobs, Theodore. 1991. *The Use of the Self: Countertransference and Communciation in the Analytic Situation.* Madison, CT: International University Press.

Jarrett, Susan C. 1991. *Feminism and Composition: The Case for Conflict Contending with Words,* edited by Patricia Harkin and John Schilb, 105–23. New York: MLA.

Kameen, Paul. 1995. "Studying Professionally: Pedagogical Relationships at the Graduate Level." *College English* 57: 448-60.

Kolodny, Annette. 1985. "A Map for Rereading: Gender and the Interpretation of Literary Texts." In *The New Feminist Criticism: Essays on Women, Literature, and Society,* edited by Elaine Showalter, 46–62. New York: Pantheon.

Kottler, Jeffrey. 1993. *On Being a Therapist.* San Francisco: Jossey-Bass.

Kraemer, Don J. Jr. 1992. "Gender and the Autobiographical Essay: A Critical Extension of the Research." *College Composition and Communication* 43 (October): 322–39.

Lindemann, Erika. 1995. *A Rhetoric for Writing Teachers.* 3d ed. New York: Oxford University Press.

Lopate, Philip. 1989. "What Happened to the Personal Essay?" In *The Fourth Genre: Contemporary Writers of/on Creative Nonfiction,* edited by Robert Root Jr. and Michael Steinberg. Boston: Allyn and Bacon, 1999.

Mairs, Nancy. 1997. *Voice Lessons: On Becoming a (Woman) Writer.* Boston: Beacon.

Malcolm, Janet. 1980. *Psychoanalysis: The Impossible Profession.* New York: Vintage.

Mitcham, Judson. 1996. "The Signature of God." *In Short: A Collection of Brief Creative Nonfiction,* 131–32. New York: Norton.

Moffett, James. 1999. "Response: Spiritual Sites of Composing." In *Writing, Teaching, Learning: A Sourcebook,* edited by Richard L. Graves, 314–20. Portsmouth, NH: Heinemann Boynton/Cook.

Mukhi, Sunita Sunder. 1996. "Guess Who's Coming to Dinner: The Second Generation Is Most Anxiety Ridden Over Dating." *Little India* (May). (http://206.20.14.67/achal/archive/may96/dating1.htm)

Murphy, Richard J. Jr. 1993. *The Calculus of Intimacy: A Teaching Life.* Columbus: Ohio State University Press.

Newkirk, Thomas. 1997. *The Performance of Self in Student Writing.* Portsmouth, NH: Heinemann Boynton/Cook.

Ngo, Anna Hang. 1995. "The Dangerous Journey." In *Fresh Ink: Essays from Boston College's First-Year Writing Seminar.* Vol. 2, 37–40. New York: McGraw-Hill College Custom.

O'Connor, Flannery. 1953. "A Good Man Is Hard to Find." In *The Story and Its Writer: An Introduction to Short Fiction,* edited by Ann Charters, 658–69. Compact 6th ed. Boston: Bedford St. Martins, 2003.

O'Reilley, Mary Rose. 1993. *The Peaceable Classroom.* Portsmouth, NH: Heinemann Boynton/Cook.

Orwell, George. 1936. "Shooting an Elephant." In *One Hundred Great Essays,* edited by Robert DiYanni, 569–76. New York: Penguin Academics, 2002.

Peterson, Linda H. 1991. "Gender and the Autobiographical Essay: Research Perspectives, Pedagogical Practices." *College Composition and Communication* 42 (May): 170–83.

Phillips, Adam. 1993. *On Tickling, Kissing, and Being Bored: Psychoanalytic Essays on the Unexamined Life.* Cambridge: Harvard University Press.

Postman, Neil, and Charles Weingartner. 1969. *Teaching as a Subversive Activity.* New York: Dell.

Rankin, Libby. 1994. *Seeing Yourself as a Teacher: Conversations with Five New Teachers in a University Writing Program.* Urbana, IL: NCTE.

Roen, Duane H. 1992. "Gender and Teacher Response to Student Writing." In *Gender Issues in the Teaching of English,* edited by Nancy Mellin

McCracken and Bruce C. Appleby, 126–41. Portsmouth, NH: Heinemann Boynton/Cook.

Root, Robert Jr., and Michael Steinberg. 1999. *The Fourth Genre: Contemporary Writers of/on Creative Nonfiction*. Boston: Allyn and Bacon.

Rose, Mike. 1989. *Lives on the Boundary: The Struggles and Achievements of America's Underprepared*. New York: Free Press.

Scholes, Robert. 1989. *Protocols of Reading*. New Haven: Yale University Press.

———. 1985. *Textual Power: Literary Theory and the Teaching of English*. New Haven: Yale University Press.

Sedaris, David. 2000. *Me Talk Pretty One Day*. Boston: Back Bay.

Sheridan, Daniel. 1991. "Changing Business as Usual: Reader Response in the Classroom." *College English* 53 (7): 804–14.

Sims, Norman, ed. 1984. *The Literary Journalists*. Reissue ed. New York: Ballantine.

Sinclair, John David. 1982. "How the Mind Recharges Batteries." *Psychology Today* 16 (November): 96.

Sirc, Geoffrey. 1989. "Gender and 'Writing Formations' in First-Year Narratives." *Freshman English News* 18 (Fall): 4–11.

Thorne, Barrie. 1993. *Gender Play: Girls and Boys in School*. New Brunswick, NJ: Rutgers University Press.

Tobin, Lad. 1993. *Writing Relationships: What Really Happens in the Composition Class*. Portsmouth, NH: Heinemann Boynton/Cook.

———. 1991. "Reading Students, Reading Ourselves: Revising the Teacher's Role in the Writing Class." *College English* 53 (7): 333–48.

Tompkins, Jane. 1996. *A Life in School: What the Teacher Learned*. Reading, MA: Addison-Wesley.

———. 1990. "Pedagogy of the Distressed." *College English* 52 (6): 653–60.

Woolf, Virginia. 1929. *A Room of One's Own*. Reissue ed. New York: Harvest Books, 1989.